The Money Minders

In the crises of the past fifteen years, central bankers have become big public players in dramas that affect all our lives, including financial market crashes, public health threats and devastating economic downturns. Having played a lead role in the global financial crisis and the coronavirus pandemic, they are now being asked to broaden their portfolio of responsibilities. But their fundamental aim has always been one of simply ensuring monetary and financial stability. In this book, Jagjit S. Chadha opens up the world of central banking, explaining in accessible language the analytical techniques, policy toolkits and simple storytelling central bankers use to understand the economy, implement monetary policy and communicate their decisions to key decision makers and the wider public.

JAGJIT S. CHADHA is Director of the National Institute of Economic and Social Research (NIESR). Previously, he was Professor of Economics at the University of Kent, at the University of Cambridge, and at the University of St Andrews. He has worked at the Bank of England on Monetary Policy, as Chief Quantitative Economist at BNP Paribas, and served as the Mercers' Memorial Professor of Commerce at Gresham College from 2014 to 2018. In 2021, he was awarded an OBE for his services to Economics and Economic Policy.

The Money Minders

The Parables, Trade-Offs and Lags of Central Banking

JAGJIT S. CHADHA

National Institute of Economic and Social Research

CAMBRIDGE
UNIVERSITY PRESS

University Printing House, Cambridge CB2 8BS, United Kingdom

One Liberty Plaza, 20th Floor, New York, NY 10006, USA

477 Williamstown Road, Port Melbourne, VIC 3207, Australia

314–321, 3rd Floor, Plot 3, Splendor Forum, Jasola District Centre, New Delhi – 110025, India

103 Penang Road, #05–06/07, Visioncrest Commercial, Singapore 238467

Cambridge University Press is part of the University of Cambridge.

It furthers the University's mission by disseminating knowledge in the pursuit of education, learning, and research at the highest international levels of excellence.

www.cambridge.org
Information on this title: www.cambridge.org/9781108838610
DOI: 10.1017/9781108975414

First published 2022

A catalogue record for this publication is available from the British Library.

Library of Congress Cataloging-in-Publication Data
Names: Chadha, Jagjit, author.
Title: The money minders : the parables, trade–offs and lags of central banking / Jagjit Chadha, National Institute for Economic and Social Research.
Description: Cambridge, United Kingdom ; New York, NY : Cambridge University Press, 2022. | Includes bibliographical references and index.
Identifiers: LCCN 2021026887 (print) | LCCN 2021026888 (ebook) | ISBN 9781108838610 (hardback) | ISBN 9781108971812 (paperback) | ISBN 9781108975414 (epub)
Subjects: LCSH: Banks and banking, Central. | Monetary policy. | Economic policy. | BISAC: BUSINESS & ECONOMICS / Economics / Macroeconomics
Classification: LCC HG1811 .C4775 2022 (print) | LCC HG1811 (ebook) | DDC 332.1/1–dc23
LC record available at https://lccn.loc.gov/2021026887
LC ebook record available at https://lccn.loc.gov/2021026888

ISBN 978-1-108-83861-0 Hardback
ISBN 978-1-108-97181-2 Paperback

Contents

Figures

Preface

Somewhere in the centre of a space that contains economics, history and politics lies a need for the state to control the value of money. The competence of the government and its central bank at this intersection seems to signal something quite important about the overall capacity of a state to deal with its collective problems. The signal of a failed state seems to be closely tied up with the collapse in confidence in its monetary and financial system; so much so that some consider sound money to be the ultimate public good – supplied by the state but of use to all private agents in their ongoing attempt to make plans for a future hampered by much risk and uncertainty. This is as much true in the year of lockdown and COVID-19 as it was during the financial crisis some dozen years ago, as well as the plethora of fluctuations in economic activity that central banks are called upon to judge the appropriate policy response.

Dull as it seems to most, money has fascinated me since, as a child, I tried to understand the move to decimal coinage from old shillings and pence and looked at the pamphlets and information films that explained the change. As I recall, the old coins looked a lot more interesting with florins and crowns minted in ancient years beating new pence hands down. But really I could not understand why it mattered so much and tried to explain to an audience of kind, but probably very bored, school parents how currency was just another way of counting, in order to win an English Speaking Board certificate. Mrs Keeley, our elderly neighbour whose supply of humbugs never seemed to run out, did understand better: these were the coins associated with Great Britain, and these new valueless coins were part of a country whose position was similarly depreciated. I did not, of course, begin to understand what she meant. In this introduction to monetary policymaking I am mostly motivated by the technical rather than the political; it pays to bear in mind the importance of the value of money to the notion of the state.

The intellectual story of monetary policymaking is one that, surprisingly, I cannot find anywhere in terms of its basic concepts. Of course, there are many financial histories and central banking histories, and the daily grind of whether interest rates are too high or too low occupies us so fully that many think these judgements are the sum total of what economists actually do. It is an occupational hazard I now wear with some humour, but after the ubiquitous discussion on house prices (in the United Kingdom, at least), conversation quickly turns to my view on interest rates.

Although I actually have always known next to nothing – as many would say that is the way it should be – about the next step in policy rates, it is the only time that people ever seem to listen to me. And this may be in part because there is no clear guide, as far as I can tell, to the principles that structure monetary policy debate. So in this short book, I take on the heroic task of filling that gap.

But what I try to do is to spell out some of the little models, folk theorems and perhaps even parables that I think most central bankers have in their toolkits – grinding away and turning with the crunch of data revelations; or what I prefer to think of as their ongoing conversations and shared judgements with markets, politicians and the public. Central bankers have at their core an understanding of trade-offs and the difficult lags inherent to any policy decision. But most of all they agree that nobody can be sure they understand tidal patterns governing economic developments and, even with those models and judgements, they are prone to considerable error, so that caution becomes both a mantra and a first response to all events.

Acknowledgements

I have so many people to thank for helping me to write this book. From my earliest formal teachers of economics, Laurie Benge and Raymond Cobb, to Chris Heady, Wendy Carlin, Michael Stewart, Negley Harte, Charles Goodhart, Mary Morgan and Morris Perlman, and, latterly, to Robin Matthews and Brian Reddaway. And then to my many co-authors who have taught me so much: Norbert Janssen, Joe Ganley, Suzanne Hudson, Andy Haldane, Francis Breedon, Philip Schellekens, Charles Nolan, Nicholas Dimsdale, Lucio Sarno, Elisa Newby, Sean Holly, Hamid Sabourian, Peter Macmillan, Katsuyuki Shibayama, Philip Turner, Lucio Sarno, Luisa Corrado, Alain Durré, Mike Joyce, Ryland Thomas, Fabrizio Zampolli, Richard Barwell and Mick Grady.

I have also learnt just as much from my students (this should surprise no one who has taught), especially Chris Brown, Tom Bradbury, Jack Meaning, Alex Waters and James Warren, with whom I have developed many of the thoughts in this book. The very kind and forgiving Council of Gresham College gave me time and space to develop many of these ideas in a series of lectures given over 2014–2015. I am grateful to have had the regular, wise advice of Richard Evans, whose taste in football teams, though, is rather questionable. And since 2016 I have been lucky enough to observe the waves of quite astonishing economics news wash over the country from 2 Dean Trench Street, off Smith Square, in Westminster, as Director of the National Institute of Economic and Social Research. My colleagues Arno Hantzsche, Jason Lennard, Garry Young, Roger Farmer, Peter Dolton, Adrian Pabst, Hande Kucuk and Paul Mortimer-Lee have often corrected many of my misapprehensions. My three chairs of council, Tim Besley, Nick Crafts and Diane Coyle, as well as trustees, in the form of David Greenaway, Paul Tucker,

Stephen King, Tera Allas, Romesh Vaitilingam, Alan Budd and Neil Gaskell, have all been equally supportive. I especially want to thank the openness and generosity of the community of economists interested in abstract notions of money, starting with the wonderful Philip Arestis, Alec Chrystal and Peter Sinclair of the Money Study Group and Forrest Capie and Geoffrey Wood of the Monetary History Group. I am also grateful to my editors at Cambridge University Press, Phil Good, Chris Harrison and Dhivyabharathi Elavazhagan.

My first and last teachers have been my parents, Mohan and Manjit, and my wife, Sahar, and most recently my children, Nihal and Jasleen. Thank you.

I   Of Gold and Paper Money

*In which I consider the role of money as a means of payment, store of value
and medium of exchange. To help fix a few ideas I outline a number of
quantitative and qualitative experiences of monetary management.
Successful regimes, that facilitate the roles, have sprung up in a variety of
surprising places, and been sustained with state (centralised) interventions.
Although the link between state and money, and its standard of identity and
account may be clear, particularly in earlier stages of economic development,
the extent to which the state is widely felt to hold responsibility for 'sound
money' is less clear in modern democracies, where there are many other
public responsibilities implying an ongoing set of issues.*

Money is not, properly speaking, one of the subjects of commerce; but
only the instrument which men have agreed upon to facilitate the
exchange of one commodity for another. It is none of the wheels of trade:
It is the oil which renders the motion of the wheels more smooth and
easy. If we consider any one kingdom by itself, it is evident, that the
greater or less plenty of money is of no consequence; since the prices of
commodities are always proportioned to the plenty of money.

David Hume, *Of Money*, 1752.

I.I   WHY MIND MONEY[1]

Maintaining a credible form of money is central to the organisation of
society. Money can take many forms and can be an actual precious
metal, and hence a commodity, or a paper version that may or may
not be linked to the value of a commodity and increasingly just an
electronic chit. In this chapter I shall discuss the development of
money, the fascination with gold and the reasons why we still need
money to perform its roles in providing operational units of account,

---

[1] A version of this chapter was given as a keynote address at the MMF Annual
Conference at Kings College London in September 2017 and an earlier version was
also given as my inaugural lecture at Gresham College on 18th September 2014, on
the night of the (first) Scottish referendum on independence. An earlier version
appeared in the Manchester School in 2018 as part of the Money, Macro Finance
Study Group Special issue. I am grateful for comments from colleagues, seminar
participants and students at the University of Kent and University of Cambridge.

means of exchange and a store of value. What we shall see is that sorting out money is one of the most important things any government, dictator or, even builder of a nation state ought to fix. In this sense money might be thought to be the ultimate public good that provides critical social capital and enables the exchange of ideas, goods and transfers of resources.[2]

As Hume hints, money, coins and even stamps represent value and a claim on goods and services. And many of us will remember looking in wonder at the many different denominations of coloured notes from childhood travels and, perhaps, wondering why they were so many types. Older readers may recall the decimalisation of sterling in February 1971: nothing and yet everything seemed to change as decimal modernity crowded out tanners and ten bob notes.[3] In fact, what might have been more important was that the world's most important currency, the US dollar, was about to end its formal link to gold in August 1971. That act finally meant we had entered the era of fiat money, that is, money which is determined by acts and deeds or promises rather than being backed by the value of an ancient commodity.

Long before money, its rate of return (which is simply the rate at which money loses its value against a basket of goods and services, otherwise known as inflation) and its opportunity cost (the interest rate that is lost by holding money rather than income-producing assets) dominated our national agenda, it had a more prosaic aim – simply to facilitate accounting and trade. The need for some uniformity in the value of money was pretty clear, as was people's ability to spot value, and so beware any debaser in case they fell afoul of Gresham's Law, which is typically expressed as 'bad money drives out good'. People have always been pretty good at working out value and Thomas Gresham spotted that if two coins, which are both legal tender, have the same nominal or face value but different values of

---

[2] See Dasgupta (2005) on this point.

[3] With 20 shillings of 12 old pence to a pound, a tanner represented half a shilling or 6 old pence. A ten bob note was half a pound with a bob being a shilling. See Feaveryear (1931) for more on these 'lost' terms.

actual commodity content, then the one that has the largest discount between its face value and actual commodity content will drive out usage of the one that has less of a difference between its face value and the actual commodity content.

The man who was the founder of the Royal Exchange, when envoy to Queen Elizabeth I, realised that people will be smart enough to work out, as had Copernicus before him, that they might be able to use 'bad' money for the purchases and keep or save the 'good' money for their nest eggs (see Shrimplin, 2017). But I think with the continuing emphasis of words like standard and sterling, the ultimate idea behind the development of commodity backing surely was simply to create money that could be trusted to hold its value and allow correct inference on the value of goods over time in terms of other goods. So it is the role of money in allowing trade to be separated in time and (geographical) space that makes its essential to the understanding of modern life.[4]

What I try to do is compress a large amount of historical time into a small number of episodes or short stories, if you will, mostly with a happy ending. These stories provide parable or heuristics that we might use to think about the further developments of money. I will also consider a number of standard problems that money is designed to solve and then summarise the implications of a well-known model from modern economics that has proved very useful for thinking about money; money springs up in this model as a solution that avoids autarchy, starvation and an unnecessarily painful old age. First let us look at some indicators of monetary performance over the long run and in and out of regimes that were related to commodity standards.

1.2   PRICES, INTEREST RATES AND MONEY

Before we consider some historical developments and experiments in money, I would like to fix some simple stylised facts, which sit in the

---

[4] Spufford (1988) provides a masterly account of these issues.

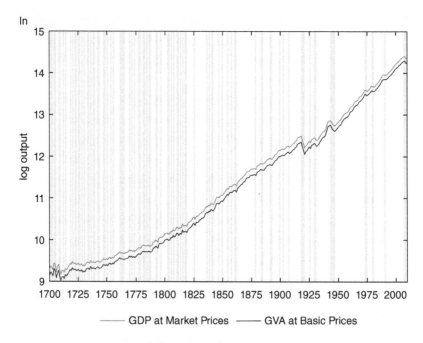

FIGURE I.I Annual chronology of British business cycles, 1700–2010
Note: Shaded areas represent recessions.

collective conscience. These 'facts' are well known to central bankers but do deserve wider exposure. If we take output to be a measure of overall welfare in the economy, monetary policy is concerned not so much with its level or its long-run growth rate but the fluctuations around those long-run tendencies, which we tend to think of or refer to as business cycles. These fluctuations occur often and with considerable irregularity, as Figure 1.1 shows in the long run for the United Kingdom. Annoyingly, much of the fluctuation may be quite acceptable but much may not so we cannot be sure as to whether we should flatten or ignore it.

Let us next ask what happens to the change in the prices of goods and services not on the year-to-year basis that dominates the current pursuit of monetary stability but on an average basis over ten years. This is so we can get to grips with what levels of inflation people might reasonably have expected or experienced over a medium-term planning horizon. We are fortunate in the United

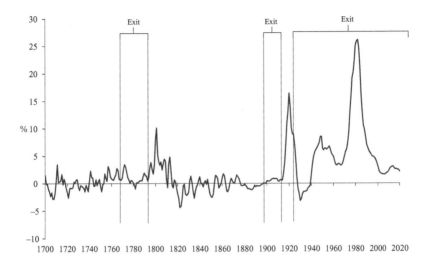

FIGURE 1.2 UK price inflation over the long run

Kingdom to be able to use data that allows us to examine broad trends in decennial inflation from the late seventeenth century, with appropriate splicing, to date.[5] Figure 1.2 shows that ten-year average inflation seems low and stable in the commodity standard periods, so much so that households and other economic agents may well not have concerned themselves with changes in the price level over the long run.

Indeed, J. M. Keynes (1923) put it rather well:

> The course of events during the nineteenth century favoured such ideas [as price stability] ... the remarkable feature of this long period was the relative *stability* of the price level. Approximately the *same* level of price ruled in or about the years 1826, 1841, 1855, 1862, 1867, 1871 and 1915. Prices were also level in the years 1844, 1881 and 1914 ... No wonder that we came to believe in the stability of money contracts over a long period.

Yet we can see that when shocks were likely to be have been large and uncertainty heightened, an 'escape clause' (Bordo and Kydland, 1992)

---

[5] See Dimsdale et al. (2010) for further details.

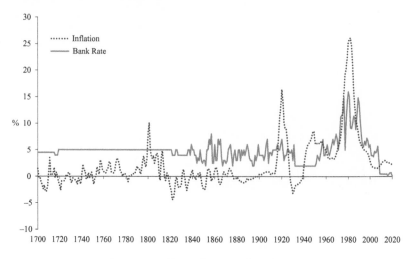

FIGURE 1.3   Ten-year rolling inflation and Bank Rate

was exercised with temporary delinking of money from its direct backing with gold in 1797–1821 and in the period around WWI. The period following the probable terminal end of the US dollar's link to gold has been characterised by persistent inflation and attempts, with varying degrees of success, at its moderation. This achievement raises the question of why does linking money to a gold or commodity standard deliver a stable price level, and why might a government or central bank consider delinking from something that seems able to guarantee some certainty in the price level when times become uncertain?

Let us now examine in Figure 1.3 what that inflation series looks like compared to Bank Rate over the same period (note though that we are mixing our horizons because a policy interest rate is typically a short-run rate and the inflation rate here is measured as a long-run average). What we note is that under the commodity standards the return on short-run interest rates, which are closely linked to those rates obtained in money markets generally, tended to be greater than long-run inflation, so that agents could reasonably expect strongly positive returns. In fact with long-run inflation broadly zero in this period, the nominal and real interest rates were, in effect, very much the same. The distinction between nominal prices, the cash return or requirement to buy an item and its real, or relative, price, compared to other goods and services, is a crucial distinction as it is changes in relative prices that typically provide a signal to people to change their behaviour. By conflating nominal and real interest rates in a zero inflation world, the central bank does not have to concern itself with explaining the distinction to markets, firms and households. Whether central banks always want to provide clarity in the game they run against economics agents is an issue to which macroeconomics regularly returns, as will I.

If savings in financial instruments that were closely linked to policy rates could deliver a positive real return, what about fluctuations in the price of gold in the long run? Does the price of gold rise inexorably with population and income because the supply is more or less fixed? At least for the benefit of any gold bugs, who seem to be large in number and vocal in noise, we might carefully examine the relative price of gold in terms of goods and services (we do this in terms of an index so that we can broadly relate to the change value, based to the sterling price of gold at the turn of the millennium). Hardly surprisingly, when the money was directly linked to gold at a given price, if the long-run price level of goods and services was broadly stable, which is a measure of the purchasing power of money, then gold prices would also not fluctuate. If money was overissued and devalued against gold, people would be inclined to hold gold instead and swap notes for gold, this would take notes out of circulation and act against the over issue and threaten the central bank's gold reserves. Maintaining gold convertibility was fundamentally important and nothing should thus threaten the exhaustion of reserves. The gold standard was essentially a statement that a fixed quantity of money could be converted to gold and that a weight of gold could be considered money: this mutually binding constraint meant that neither gold nor money could fluctuate in price very much, as we see in Figure 1.3

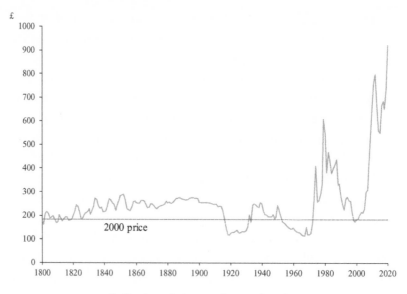

FIGURE 1.4 Gold price relative to other goods and services

In a standard textbook model (e.g. Barro, 1979), a commodity standard is simply a statement that a given quantity of a commodity, for example, a standard ounce of gold, can always be exchanged for a set quantity of domestic currency. In the United Kingdom, Isaac Newton as Master of Mint in 1717 set the ratio as £3.17s.10½d; secondly, that the quantity of domestic currency in issue is limited by some ratio to gold held in reserves at the central bank. Therefore, under the gold standard, money is in effect circulating as claims on gold. The quantity of the medium is constrained by the quantity of monetary gold and the perceived degree to which the issue needs to be backed. As the quantity of money is fixed by the supply of monetary gold and the price is fixed by the exchange rate with gold, there would appear to have been a considerable degree of automatic monetary stability. Furthermore, if other countries' currencies are also linked to gold, we end up with a de facto international system of fixed exchange rates in terms of the gold prices of each currency. This not only served us well but became folksy homeland to which many still pay homage.

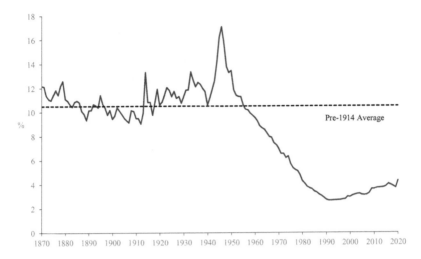

FIGURE 1.5 Narrow money to income ratio

In this context we can then try to understand the propensity of people to hold narrow money, notes and coins, relative to national income, shown in Figure 1.5. Under the earlier stable price period, the rate of return of money was broadly zero and remained a stable proportion of income. Many economists (starting perhaps with Goodhart and Crockett, 1970) have tried to understand what drives the demand for money, and in general the resulting models reflect some view that money is required to finance current expenditures and provides insurance, in terms of liquidity, against unanticipated shifts in income. What we can also see is that when inflation became positive and persistent, the demand for money began a long secular decline. With a negative rate of return on holding money, even if income is growing and liquidity is still an important consideration, people simply have a great propensity to economise, increasingly so, on narrow money balances.

Broadly speaking, what we see from these charts is quite challenging. Commodity monies seemed to deliver greater inflation (a.k.a. price) stability and short-term assets seemed to provide a positive hedge against any inflation, so that real rates of interest were consistently positive, the real gold price was stable and there was a stable demand for the notes and coins when compared to income. Given the long backdrop of wars, industrialisation and the development of modernity, any monetary stability was remarkable. And at least at first blush, the subsequent absence of monetary stability looks equally as stark.

And yet after the financial crisis of 2007–2008, which has been of enormous import in the new world of ongoing monetary and financial reform, no one serious thinks – quite rightly – that we ought to return to a commodity standard. Let me see if we can move towards a resolution of this puzzle. The answer lies not so much with the certainties introduced by a commodity standard where the price level is fixed in terms of a given quantity of precious metal, unless there are large enough shocks. But once society developed a theory and then a responsibility for the government of the quarter-to-quarter and year-to-year performance of the economy, this 'barbarous relic' of a gold standard was done for (Keynes, 1923). Such responsibilities simply cannot be discharged with a fixed price regime. Indeed the short-run volatility in prices from such a regime may itself generate much in the way of unwarranted economic fluctuations.[6]

1.3   SOME PARABLES

Let us move swiftly over time and space: a central banker looks for foundations and building blocks to build his or her theoretical world, or model. Naturally, as the statistician G. E. P. Box may or may not have said: 'all models are wrong, but some are useful'. Let us see if we can find something useful from the lessons of history. We shall look at the development of the first standard coins in ancient Lydia and note the power that this gave to the issuer. We shall then move back and south to Mesopotamia and try to understand how credit evolved to

---

[6] See Chadha and Sarno (2002) for an examination of annual inflation volatility (or uncertainty) under the gold standard, which was surprisingly high compared to post-war regimes.

help communities deal with shocks. Given that credit was directed by the state, I wonder whether credit was the first monetary policy. Then we move onto Song dynasty China, where notes replaced cash and were so instrumental in allowing trade to expand. Standards returned in eighteenth-century England but by Newtonian accident. The increasingly important state also discovered that it could temporarily tamper with monetary standards and not only get away with it but promote greater prosperity than would otherwise have been obtained. Even when money disappears and trade is nearly extinguished, for example, in a prisoner-of-war camp, commodities can spring up and become money. We find that economic and political unions require a common currency, or is it the other way around, in the form of the Act of Union in 1707?

I.4 CROESUS

The first historian, Herodotus, tells us the story of the man who had been the wealthiest man in the ancient world, King Croesus of Lydia. Apart from a morality tale about the difference between wealth and happiness, richly illustrated by heartrending ultimate sadness, Herodotus tells us much about money. Croesus' wealth and that of Lydia stemmed not only from the naturally occurring alloys of silver and gold, electrum, but even more so from the ability to separate the alloy using a chemical process involving common salt, that allowed coins of pure gold and silver to be minted. These coins were stamped with symbols and because they moved the valuation problem from the trader to the ruler, they allowed the Lydians to develop unchallenged financial power with their gold coins acting as the ancient world's reserve currency. Perhaps the ultimate source of this financial power was simply trust in the coinage. In an imaginary scene, a recent novel outlined a conversation between Croesus and his father, Alyattes:[7]

---

[7] Leach, pp. 84–85.

'Can I tell you a secret?' Alyattes pointed at the image of the lion. 'Without that stamp, it is valued at whatever some metal trader tells you it is worth. With that mark, it's worth as much as *I* say it is worth.' ... 'It's harvest season now. The farmers are gathering their wheat from the land.' He reached out a finger and tapped the metal disc in Croesus' palm. 'If I say so, one of these coins will buy the crop of a poor farmer's field. Forty of them and you've got the worth of everything that farmer will ever produce. The entire value of a common man's life ...'

The benefits arising from seigniorage become manifest. In this way, this first global money heralded the modern age by facilitating trade but also warned of the excesses and disasters that may follow from unfettered, centralised power. It possibly also hinted at the regular problems that economics has with the theory of value and exchange – how can one man at one instant and by accident of birth or luck of discovery own the entire lifetime real output of so many other men? The tension between the financial and real sectors remains.

I.5   BABYLONIAN LOAN CONTRACTS

The development of Babylonian mathematics (in base 60), facilitated the calculation of interest over time, and alongside that of the written word, allowed records of loan and credit markets to develop as early as the fourth millennium BC.[8] Exchanges of goods and services in an increasingly specialised economy took place at first in a temple and then at the palace – from spiritual to regal. From such markets, which one can think of as a general store, rations were issued to consumers in sizes ordered by the gender, age and importance of the subject. These rations were 'backed' by donations made by producers, such

---

[8] See chapter 1, 'The Invention of Interest – Sumerian Loans' by Marc Mieroop in Goetzmann and Rouwenhorst (2005).

as farmers and fisherman. Given that demand might be considered as set in advance and forecastable, it was probably negative shocks to production that lead to arrears and the need to borrow from others. A wise custodian may have promoted the build-up of inventories in good years. Interest rates on loans were some 20 per cent for silver and 33 per cent for barley, probably because barley was demanded before harvest and paid back afterwards when the price was likely to be lower. Without money, credit by way of clay tablets was used to record claims on producers and these claims were traded: Babylonian asset backed securities, if you will. Once a contract was settled, the tablet was soaked in water and the clay ready to be reused, as the 'slate was wiped clean'. The remaining tablets are thus arch-aeological remnants of failed loans. Sometimes failure leaves more of a lasting impression that success.

Under uncertainty in production, credit and loans at interest stood ready to smooth the path to consumption and these may even be thought of as the first form of monetary policy. We might think of a monetary policy as something that tries to limit inefficient fluctuations in output by using tools related to the supply of money and credit. My point is not so much that loans were some dangerous development but rather, once we decide to ration and centralise demand and production, lending between families of producers might be the only way to make the system stand firm in the face of large unanticipated shifts in supply by individual farmers. An absence of credit, in these conditions, may have threatened social stability. In this sense, credit and debt are simply ways of sharing risk when not all news, or shocks, hit every household in the same way.

1.6   PAPER MONEY DURING THE SONG DYNASTY

By the third century BC, money had pretty much become fundamental to economic exchange in China, but rather than the precious metals favoured in the West, the imperial monetary system was based on bronze.[9] It was in China that the first viable paper currency was developed, as well as the fiat bronze coin. Echoing the (imagined) words of the Lydians, 'Chinese philosophers and statesman ... have universally asserted that money is an artefact of the supreme ruling authority. It is the ruler's stamp, not the intrinsic value of the monetary medium, that confers value.' The Song dynasty was founded in 960 and absorbed other kingdoms but there was a chronic shortage of bronze coin, which was the means by which tax was paid. The parallel iron currency did not help much and merchants' exchange bills (jiaozi) began to circulate. These bills proliferated in a chaotic manner and the right to issue was eventually restricted to sixteen merchant houses by Zhang Young in 1005, the prefect of Chengdu, with standardised size and colour.

The merchants who had issued jiaozi held their own assets in (illiquid) land and luxury commodities, leaving the merchant houses vulnerable to a liquidity shock. To add to the monetary problems, significant quantities of counterfeits started to enter circulation. By 1023/4 the incoming prefect, Xue Tian, created a state-run currency bureau which issued notes in both restricted denomination and limited life. The note issue had to expand with the requirements for trade but in a credible manner so that the quantity of notes had some limit to their issuance as did, in this case, their life expectancy. Technology also underpinned the invention of paper money, as paper-making and printing used Mulberry paper and metal printing plates. The records allow us to observe a rapid increase in the issue and circulation of these notes with no deleterious effects on the value of money with 10mn guan in circulation c. 1170 and some 270mn in circulation by the middle of the following century. In other words, in order to create money of value, it was not simply that supply had to be tightly regulated but also that it had to be carefully expanded to meet growing demand. Issuers of paper are confronted with the ever-present

---

[9] See chapter 4, 'The Origins of Paper Money in China' by Richard von Glahn in Goetzmann and Rouwenhorst (2005).

possibility that growing quantities of money in circulation may either reflect success with demand reflecting a growing economy or be undermining belief in the stability of the currency's value.[10]

1.7   NEWTON'S GAFFE

One of the foremost intellectuals of his (or any other) day sat in his office at the Tower of London and thought hard about the correct value of money. His preferred monetary standard, silver, was becoming increasingly scarce and it was his responsibility to try and correct this matter. Gold coins were driving silver ones out of domestic existence. The question he was wrestling with was whether he could use available empirical evidence to formulate an equation that could be used to pin down the correct value of silver and thus save it as the circulating medium. He had famously accomplished this kind of task with no little success in his earlier incarnation as Lucasian Professor of Mathematics at Cambridge; after leaving Cambridge in 1696, Sir Isaac Newton had become Warden of the Mint and succeeded as Master of the Mint in 1699, a post he held until his death in 1727. As well as spending much of his time dealing with counterfeiting, he had to ensure that the correct quantity of coins circulated to match the demands of industry and finance.[11]

At this time both silver and gold circulated as money, but silver was set at a price in Britain that undervalued it in terms of gold relative to the value placed on it on the Continent by a small margin and relative to the East by an incredible margin. The unit of account was the Guinea which has been valued at 21s and 6d since 1699 (see Findlay Shirras and Craig, 1945). In July 1702 Newton notes to Godolphin that gold is higher in France by around 9d or 10d in the Guinea; than in Holland by 11d or 12 pence in the Guinea; than in

[10] The issue of whether money growth reflects the demands of business or is inflationary is related to the question of the whether notes or bills 'are lent in exchange for "real bills", i.e. titles to real value or value in the process of creation' (Green, 1989).

[11] Levenson (2009) provides a hugely enjoyable telling of the tale.

Germany and Italy by 12d in the Guinea or above. In Spain and Portugal gold is higher than in England by about 11d in the Guinea, which implies a relative undervaluation of around 1/21 or just under 5 per cent, given 21 silver shillings in a Guinea. Later in September 1717, he notes that in China and Japan one pound weight of fine gold is worth but nine or ten pounds weight of fine silver, and in East India may be worth twelve. This low price of gold in proportion to silver carries away all the silver from all of Europe. He was clearly aware that different relative prices of gold in terms of silver were leading to international flows of silver to where it was valued most highly; these flows were exploiting the differential in silver values by a form of 'round-tripping'. That is, English importers of goods from the Continent with bills to pay in foreign currencies linked to both gold and silver would choose to remit silver, which was more valuable there in terms of gold, rather than sending gold itself.

In September 1717, Newton, as Master of the Mint, had been asked by the Lords Commissioners of His Majesty's Treasury to decide the correct rate of exchange between the two. He could devalue gold to fewer shillings (s) per Guinea and match the European price, which typically implied an exchange rate somewhere below 21s. However, he decided to set the exchange at 21 silver shillings for a Guinea of British gold, which itself was priced in terms of domestic currency at £3.17s.10½d per standard ounce, and meant that silver was worth more abroad in terms of gold than here and so it flew away. Whilst the gold standard is typically dated to have started then, it is reasonably clear that it was not designed as such by Newton and its ultimate longevity 'was largely inadvertent'.[12] Apart from two war-time suspensions from 1797 to 1819, and again with the breakdown of the gold standard during World War I followed by the resumption from 1925 to 1931, this price of gold remained fixed until 1931.[13] Compare that fixed price to the barely twenty-three months that

---

[12] See Kindleberger, p. 57, on this point.
[13] There had been a minor suspension in 1745 as a result of the Jacobite invasion.

sterling managed to stay pegged to the Deutschmark from October 1990 to September 1992.

Newton realised that:

> if things be left alone till silver money be a little scarcer, the Gold will fall of itself. For people are already backward to give Silver for Gold, and will in a little time refuse to make payments in Silver without a premium, as they do in Spain, and this premium with an abatement in the value of Gold shall be lowered by the government, or let alone till it falls of itself by the want of silver money.

He foresaw further devaluations of gold in order to bring increasingly scarce silver back into circulation. What he did not foresee nor adequately understand, is that the gold Guinea at 21s had become a prominent unit of account and means of transaction by industry, trade, banks and even tax collectors: it had become the 'standard coin', indeed a norm, and there was considerable opposition to any further devaluations.[14] The gold standard arrived because Newton's revaluation had produced a gold coin of widely useful value and simply drove silver out of circulation, so much so that by 1774 silver was demonetised. The lesson for central banks is both that custom and practice matters and that speculators are hard to beat.

1.8   TEMPORARY EXIT FROM THE GOLD STANDARD

States can be tested under extreme conditions and the monetary constitution is one of the first areas in need of attention. During the Revolutionary and Napoleonic wars, economic policy was developing at a rapid rate with large persistent deficits to fund income tax introduced. With the growth in central bank liabilities undermining the strength of support by dwindling gold reserves, suspension of gold convertibility in 1797 allowed the Bank of England to nurture British monetary orthodoxy in extreme conditions. The Order of the Privy Council's decision to suspend gold payments on Bank of

---

[14] Feavearyear, pp. 156–157.

England notes afforded simultaneous protection to the government and the bank in pursuit of the conflicting goals of price stability and war finance. The government, the Bank of England and the commercial banks formed a loose alliance drawing on due political and legal processes and also paid close attention to public opinion.[15]

In the 1790s the economy was volatile, as perhaps in any ten-year period, and this was expressed in a Canal Mania, an existential war involving high levels of government expenditure and an unlucky sequence of bad harvests. There were numerous reported sightings of French fleets and this led to some hoarding of gold by the public and country banks. As would now seem to be the custom, there were first bank runs in the North-East on 18 February 1797 and more of a panic after the reported landing of a handful of French soldiers at Fishguard on 22 February 1797. The result was that the Bank of England's gold reserve and the circulating money stock fell rapidly, as money was used to claim gold. On Saturday, 25 February an emergency Privy Council meeting was called for Sunday and King George III, the Privy Council and Pitt met in Whitehall and issued an Order of the Privy Council:

> It is the unanimous opinion of the Board, that it is indispensably necessary for the public service, that the directors of the Bank of England should forbear issuing any cash in payment until the sense of Parliament can be taken on that subject and the proper measures adopted thereupon for maintaining the means of circulation and supporting the public and commercial credit of the kingdom at this important conjuncture.
>
> *The Message from the King, 26 February 1797*

George III sent this message to the House on Monday and the bank issued notice of suspension on the same Monday morning. The Order of the Privy Council and the House of Commons tied the Bank's hands but also and fortunately, indemnified the Bank so that it could

---

[15] See Chadha and Newby (2013) for further details.

legitimately refuse to pay in gold. The Privy Council acted at the bank's suggestion and communicated to all parties simultaneously. General meetings in the City of London led to public agreement across money markets and merchants that the suspension was the right policy for as long as the war was yet to have been won.

It turned out that the ongoing solvency of the Bank of England was facilitated by suspension and allowed the bank to continue to make substantial profits throughout the wars. It became acceptable for merchants to continue to trade with non-convertible Bank of England notes and for the government to finance the war effort, even with significant recourse to unfunded debt. These aspects combined to create a suspension of convertibility that did not undermine the currency. Especially after the suspension and until eventual resumption, twelve Acts of Parliament were passed committing the monetary system to resumption.

In contrast, the French monetary experiment of the assignats had led to a debacle that cost the French monetary system its reputation. The assignats were revolutionary notes backed by confiscated land but without appropriate controls of the quantity of issuance and hence on the scale of the backing of notes by assets of value. The resulting hyperinflation in the last decade of the eighteenth century meant that Napoleonic finance had to evolve within a more rigid and limiting framework. It is possible to argue that the debate on the causes of inflation and the need to return to the gold standard, the so-called Bullionist Controversy, set up much of the intellectual framework for so-called British Monetary Orthodoxy, or what we might call Sound Money, and led to a consensus for early return to the gold standard on the cessation of hostilities as Newton's price, and at no other.

1.9 CIGARETTES

Richard Radford (1945) famously tells the story of how cigarettes became the monetary unit in an economy of several thousand prisoners of war with food rations (endowments) provided by the Red Cross at regular frequency alongside some private parcels that entered the economy from time to time. He writes, 'most trading was for food against cigarettes or other foodstuffs, but cigarettes rose from the status of a normal commodity to that of currency'. Indeed, prices adjusted and became known, 'it was realised that a tin of jam was worth 1/2 lb of margarine plus something else; that a cigarette issue was worth several chocolate issues, and a tin of diced carrots was worth practically nothing!' And so relative prices or values were known and expressed in cigarettes near universal observance. But not perfectly so, as the law of one price held particularly for food but less so for clothes, which depended on quality, age and taste.

Segmented markets were arbitraged away by skilful intermediaries: one man capitalised upon his knowledge of Urdu by buying meat from the Sikhs and selling butter and jam in return. As his operations became better known more and more people entered this trade and prices in the Indian Wing approximated to those elsewhere. One could eventually observe that spot and intra-week credit markets allowed prices for bread and treacle to be set on forward markets. Cigarettes were clipped or sweated and subject to Gresham's Law. With both monetary and non-monetary demand for cigarettes, as the time passed between the arrival of food parcels the price level would fall and be bolstered once new money arrived on a Monday morning. Arrivals of new prisoners – bringing demand for goods – would raise prices and even rumours of impending arrivals would have the same – sunspot – effect, but when reserves began to be built up, prices tended to be more stable. The money market, albeit in cigarettes, facilitated the matching of preferences and endowments at market-clearing relative prices.

1.10   THE SCOTTISH POUND

The monetary union between England and Scotland was an integral element of the economic and political union that Sidney Checkland (1975) states was 'agreed by the two Parliaments to merge as one economy, one polity and ... one society'. The Bank of England had a partial monopoly over note issue in 1708 and this was gradually extended over time with the legal tender of the English pound. A key element of monetary unions has been an agreement over debt issues and fiscal transfers. This was recognised as early as 1707, when under the Act of Union with Scotland, England agreed to pay compensation for future tax liabilities. Article 15 of the Act provided the Scots with compensation for future tax liabilities (see Clapham, 1944, p. 60); England was to pay Scotland the Equivalent: a sum of £398,085 10s sterling. The Equivalent was a capitalised valuation of the existing revenue yield from Scotland and was envisaged as a transfer from England to Scotland. Using Gregory King's estimate of national income in 1688 of around £50 million (Mitchell, 1962), this amount was equal to around 0.5–1.0 per cent of English GDP. Ultimately, however, only a small proportion of this was actually paid, in part because Exchequer Bills were not acceptable north of the border! Any reverse direction of travel will require considerable unpicking.

A story we are piecing together is that money is as much a part of our social relations as our culture and language. States large or small, federations, existing monetary unions or ones about to be born that choose to ignore the need to get the monetary constitution right, play fast and loose with the economy and also with the fabric of society. Central bankers learn to understand this innate link between the state and the need to maintain the stability of monetary exchange.

I.II   MONEY PROBLEMS

Money is supposed to be neutral as it has no impact on real output, income or expenditure or the set of relative prices that clear markets. But how can something that allows trade to be affected in the first place take no part in the final equilibrium outcome? Surely if it is valued then individuals will be prepared to pay some fraction of the goods and services they can buy with the proceeds of their labour in exchange for money?

We shall build a reply by first outlining two further key problems to which money may offer a solution. In the 1870s Jevons outlined the basic problem with barter: we need a double coincidence of wants. The person who wants to sell his goat to pay for his ale, needs to find someone who wants to sell his ale for a goat. There is a related problem of verifying that the goat is healthy and the ale is good, obviously the latter is easier than the former. If the person can find someone like this, the actual cost of trade is small because they simply meet and exchange. On the other hand if we have money in our system, the person can sell the goat to anyone who wants one, not just publicans and, armed with that money, can purchase ale from any publican, wine bar or off licence. In this case, the person pays two sets of search costs, assuming that everyone is trained to recognise money at birth or that counterfeiting does not occur in this goat–ale world. So whilst barter is simple if one can find a match, money is so very useful because it increases the number of people with whom one can trade and can also allow for some time to find the right type of ale. The more trading possibilities there are, the more useful money will be, as it increase the chance of finding a match. The person still ends up trading the goat for ale and so the exchange value is not changed; even whilst the money is neutral, the person is better off because their own notion of welfare is enhanced.

There is another form of trade impediment that monetary co-ordination can allay. In the early twentieth century, Wicksell outlined the following problem of liquidity: investor A wants to invest on Monday with her project to pay-back on Wednesday, investor B actually has money today but wants to invest on Tuesday from which she will get her money back on Thursday but cannot lend today to investor A on Monday. Investor C will get her return from a previous investment tomorrow on Tuesday but wants to start a new project on Wednesday from which she will get her money back on Friday. Although there is enough money in this system, this liquidity problem has no bilateral solution as none of A, B or C in any pair can clear their supply and demand for funds on any one day.

Imagine though that all returns from investments are pooled or deposited in a national or central bank and then made available to investors on demand. In this way, the bank will transfer money from B to A on Monday; from C to B on Tuesday; from A to C on Wednesday; from B to A on Thursday; and so on. The bank passes the deposit, or liability, to the new investor, as an asset, every day and its books balance. Naturally we hope these investors make good investment decisions on the quality and timeliness of their investments, otherwise should one transfer fail, the whole system of exchange will collapse. But again, the primitive demand for money and its supply is facilitated here rather than altered. Money remains neutral and yet a great facilitator.

I.12   SAMUELSON'S MODEL

Modern economists have developed a number of techniques for motivating money holdings in the household balance sheet. Money holdings might be held because they directly increase household utility, or because money (or cash) might be the only way households can effect transactions or money might reduce the search costs of households for goods and services. Let us understand how the young – in a model developed by Paul Samuelson (Samuelson, 1958) – can trade with the old. Imagine, if you will, an endowment economy in which a number of young people who live for two periods are given a perishable, non-storable commodity that can produce enough food for their two periods of life in a single period. Imagine in that same economy, that there are the same number of old people living alongside the young who have no endowment but will still wish to eat in their second and final period of life. How can the young 'save' the endowment for their old age and how can we get some of the endowment to the old?

There is no easy solution. If the young 'give' half their endowment to the 'old', that may solve the problem for this period via altruism, but how can the young be sure that in the next period, when they are old, the as yet unborn young will also be quite so generous? If the young keep and eat the whole endowment, they will grow rather fat in the first period of their lives and develop all kinds of cardiovascular problems that will make their old ages somewhat intolerable. A traditional answer might be to commission a benign dictator, perhaps a Lydian or a Babylonian, to capture (or sequestrate) half of the endowment and reallocate it to the old. But there is a well-known problem with trying to keep benign dictators from turning malign over time, as they tend to take a bigger cut for intermediation over time or start to seek priority reallocations to friends and family.[16] It turns out that a primary issue of fiat money, perhaps from a benign dictator who then extinguishes him or herself, is the answer.

Imagine our benign dictator issues one unit of durable money to each old person and is able to declare that this money is legal tender from now until the end of time. Armed with their units of (free) money, the current old can now trade with the current young as they swap something with the young that will be valued after their death when the young themselves become old and will have to trade with the next generation for their food. This is a remarkable result: if the state can issue something that everyone knows will be accepted and exchanged generation after generation, you can affect trade between generations and allow the old to eat and the young to save. What will happen in this case, known as the Golden Rule, is that the young will consume half of their endowment and will trade the rest with the old for money that they will use to buy half the endowment of tomorrow's young.

If we issue sufficient money to allow trade between the young and old generations at a numeraire price of 1, we may think that there is nothing much else to worry about, but only if there is no growth in the population or the endowment. If the population and/or the endowment grow every year but the quantity of money in issue is constant, the only way that a given quantity of the money stock held by the old can purchase a greater quantity of goods is if each unit of money goes further; that is, if the price level falls in proportion to the increase in goods available. If the price level falls, the rate of return

---

[16] This problem is succinctly put as 'quis custodiet ipsos custodes' in Juneval's Satires.

on money is positive and the implied interest rate on money balances is positive.

We can thus note in general terms that the price of the endowment in terms of money will be determined by the supply of money (the number of old times the number of notes) and the demand for money (the number of young times the quantity of the endowment for sale). If the population starts to grow, and with it the endowment every year, and the supply of money remains fixed, prices will start to fall and each note will start to buy more endowment. Equivalently, if the old start popping off early and take their money with them, the remaining old will have more spending power and the value of money will temporarily increase. If the benign dictator gets fat finger syndrome and issues more notes, then the price of the endowment in terms of money will rise in proportion to that issue. The price level that will clear the market for the money and the endowments simultaneously is equivalent to a return on money.

Note that some issues remain. The money must be issued in units that closely correspond to the value of items to be bought. Actually, the supply of the correct quantity of small change in a gold standard is rather tricky and the failure to address this problem may have been responsible for medieval currency debasements, as a shortage of small coins may have provided an incentive to debase the existing money supply (see Sargent and Velde, 2002). Prior to the suspension of convertibility in February 1797, the smallest Bank of England note in a circulation of just under £10mn in 1796 was £5, and at a time when a quartern loaf of bread cost somewhere between 8 and 10d, less than a shilling; so that a fiver would you bought you a gross of quartern loaves! Today's fiver would deliver around 1 3/4 quartern loaves, though naturally incomes have gone up in the intervening period. I am concerned here with prices and monetary quantities.[17]

---

[17] A quartern loaf represents four imperial pounds of bread and thus is some 1.8kg. For example, the ONS stated that 800g of bread was £1.26 in 2012. This meant that an equivalent quartern would be £2.86 and we got around 1 and three quarters of them for a fiver.

There are two further issues that also emerge from this problem. What happens if the notes change or start to disappear? In this set-up there is no incentive for old people to hoard notes because they will not be alive in the next period to spend the hoard and by doing so they will go hungry and bring forward the time of their deaths. But what if a new dictator demands 'that the notes that are blue are no longer true and the ones that are red can only be used to be fed'? Well if the dictator has a central bank that can swap the old blue notes for the new red, there may be little disruption to intertemporal trade, but if the central bank does not have enough red notes or cannot effect exchange quickly, so that the exchange has to take place over several periods, some disruption to trade will occur and the relative prices of the endowment in blue and red notes may differ, with the prices in the latter currency somewhat lower than those of the former. So Gresham's Law may even be reversed with good money driving out bad.

Finally, as any autonomous changes in the quantity of money may affect market-clearing prices, the note issuer may have an incentive to change the stock of money if the number of young being born or the quantity of the endowment for each young person changes. Of course the note issuer may wish to let the price level adjust, but it is possible to maintain stable prices by correctly anticipating changes in the demand and supply of goods. Why we might want prices to be stable is a question we leave aside for the moment, but clearly if you believe that changes in prices may lead to households holding the wrong quantity of money or admit the possibility that because of sticky price adjustment that markets may not then clear, it might be better to meet rather than frustrate expectations formed over long generational experience.

Again, in general, once we allow for demand to move and supply to respond, there will be a choice for the social planner as to whether prices can adjust to clear the market or whether the planner may need to alter the level of money in the system to bring about adjustment so that the old and young can calculate the rate of return on money.

This is very much an easier problem if the price level is always set at 1, and this is essentially the solution offered by a commodity, or gold, standard.[18]

I.I3   MONEY AND THE STATE

We consider the role of money as a means of payment, store of value and medium of exchange. I outline a number of quantitative and qualitative experiences of monetary management. Successful regimes have sprung up in a variety of surprising places and been sustained with state (centralised) interventions. Although the link between state and money and its standard of identity and account may be clear, particularly in earlier stages of economic development, the extent to which the state is widely felt to hold responsibility for 'sound money' is less clear in modern democracies, where there are many other public responsibilities implying ongoing trade-offs.

Getting money to work has been the job of the state. If money can allow trade between generations, or analogously between different types of people, then it may allow common rules to be enforced that increase everyone's welfare. Economists know quite well that there are incentives for one person to disobey common rules, on the basis that he or she will gain an advantage over the rest. But if all disobey then all will lose. The tragedy of the commons is reversed with money – the common usage of money benefits all and in this world repeated devaluation of money may be the ultimate tragedy. That is probably why the gold standard and other commodity standards persisted for so long.

In his article, Samuelson likened the Golden Rule for money to a form of Kant's Categorical Imperative, as supplying money to facilitate trade is akin to a universal maxim. Money can complete the social compact: when economists say that one of the functions of money is to act as a store of wealth and that one of money's desirable

---

[18] Of course, gold prices themselves might be affected by discoveries in supply and changes in technology.

properties is constancy of value (as measured by constancy of average prices), we are entitled to ask: how do you know this? Why *should* prices be stable? On which tablet is that injunction written? Perhaps the function of money, if it is to serve as an optimal store of wealth, is so to change its value as to create that optimal pattern of lifetime savings which could otherwise be established by alternative social contrivances.

Somewhere in the centre of a space that contains economics, history and politics there is a need for the state to control the value of money. The competence of the government in this field seems to signal something quite important about the capacity of a state to deal with its collective problems; so much so that some consider sound money to be the ultimate public good – supplied by the state but of use to all private agents in their ongoing attempt to make plans for the future hampered by so many types uncertainty. However, if the state can also help agents offset shocks when uncertainty is resolved in some dimension or other, it is not such a great intellectual leap for the state to take responsibility for economic stability.

2 The Great Depression and Its Legacy

In which we understand how the extreme fluctuations in economic activity in the interwar period led to the development of big picture or macroeconomics. And so created an obligation for the state to stabilise rather than wring its hands at economic downturns and the unemployment so created. Normative statements about what should be done rather than descriptions thus become common.

There is a line among the fragments of the Greek poet Archilochus which says: 'The fox knows many things, but the hedgehog knows one big thing.' Scholars have differed about the correct interpretation of these dark words, which may mean no more than that the fox, for all his cunning, is defeated by the hedgehog's one defence ... [T]here exists a great chasm between those, on one side, who relate everything to a single central vision, one system, less or more coherent or articulate, in terms of which they understand, think and feel – a single, universal, organising principle in terms of which alone all that they are and say has significance – and, on the other side, those who pursue many ends, often unrelated and even contradictory, connected, if at all, only in some de facto way, for some psychological or physiological cause, related to no moral or aesthetic principle.

Isaiah Berlin, *The Hedgehog and the Fox*, 1953

2.1 FROM STANDARDS TO OBLIGATIONS

The foundations of knowledge, which include language and even economics, can be subject to intellectual earthquakes.[1] Such earthquakes test the robustness of established views and may lead to previously unanticipated directions for thought. A classic example is the impact of the Great Depression on the direction of economics, as it led to the development of an obligation for the government to run

[1] I sometimes wonder whether Isaiah Berlin's separation of thought is a suitable classification to think about micro-founded macroeconomics versus the more subtle form of political economy that many seem to wish we used instead. I would like to think that such models provide a suitable single lens from which to start.

countercyclical economic policies and subsequently to the growth of national income accounting, which laid the basis for the development of macroeconomic modelling. These earthquakes expose fissures between different schools of thought, and economics continues to be torn between those who are, broadly speaking, expansionists and those who are more conservative.[2] Indeed, the spectre of the Great Depression with its images of long food queues and marchers asking for work has had a particular hold on central bank thought; so much so that at the time of the financial crisis and in its aftermath, both the Chairman of the Federal Reserve and the Governor of the Bank of the England were academic economists who had written on the events of the Great Depression.

It is now hard to turn on the TV or our tablets, or open the newspapers without some commentary on the most recent or break-ing economic story. The global financial crisis dominated headlines for the best part of a decade and will drive a generation of economists to think about the financial sector in the same way that earlier generations were driven to think about unemployment. And we are now in the middle of another crisis brought about by a global pan-demic where to some large degree the economy is even being used as an instrument to control the spread of a new virus. The crisis of COVID-19 has also exposed all transparently to the limits of monet-ary policy in that it cannot change economic structures and bring forward public goods such as health and better levels of education.

That said, it was probably during the twentieth century that the economy began to take centre stage in the public debate. A series of crises related to managing adjustment after World War I, which was called the Slump, and the Great Depression in the 1930s, promoted not only executive discussion of economic policy but also the need to collect data and explore the relevance of different theories of adjust-ment. The debates between Ralph Hawtrey, Arthur Pigou and Maynard Keynes (all Cambridge men, but in order Eton–Harrow–Eton) entered

---

[2] See, for example, Ayres (1946).

the public arena, and their echoes continue to be heard today: for the Treasury, View of Sound Money then can be replaced with the debates around Austerity today.[3] And the echoes continue to reverberate with the important debate between personal health and economic progress and asking what is the trade-off between them? It turns out that just like the Phillips curve that we discuss shortly, there is no long-term trade-off between the two.

The development of macroeconomic stabilisation policy in the middle decades of the twentieth century, which we shall consider more in the next chapter, seemed to have been a huge success during the so-called post-war Golden Age with both recovery and stability widely appreciated, but the foundations of policy had cracks that ultimately undid the post-war practice. That story is one I will deal with again in the next chapter. The near loss of monetary control in the 1970s awakened an interest in the microeconomic foundations of macroeconomic theory, which involved deriving aggregate behavioural equations from optimisation problems where agents worked out a plan that took into account the future and the present in a so-called intertemporal decision and also an intra-temporal choice that means agents would not wish to reallocate the time they spend on various activities within any period. These decision rules are also subject to an economy-wide resource, or budget constraint.

The late 20th century hope was that such models would be usable for policy analysis in terms of welfare because the fundamental relationships were stable in the face of changes in policy. Traditional economic models, which are heavily reliant on econometric estimation, were thought to fall foul of the Lucas critique.[4] Such models attached more importance to external realism with recognisable facets and not too much abstraction, rather than to internal

---

[3] In part to help with post-war reconstruction, after WWII, Pigou (1948) was commissioned to write the economic history of the immediate period after WWI and it remains a clear exposition of the classical position.

[4] I shall explain this mysterious critique in chapter 4 with the help of a footballing analogy.

coherence, as do some heterodox and agent-based approaches. In contrast, the macroeconomic models with micro-foundations that became popular in the 1990s attach more importance to internal (logical) coherence than to external realism per se, at least at first.

Let us start at the beginning of macroeconomics. The backdrop, to what I think is right to call, the Keynesian revolution, was the set of classical postulates that can be summed up with the simple view that interest rates can be moved in order to bring the demand for goods in line with its supply and hence clear the market for goods. First, output can be thought of as one of three equivalent quantities: the production of goods (supply); expenditure on those goods (demand); or income (wages, profits or rents) collected by the factors of production in the process of production. This measure came to be known as gross domestic product (GDP).[5] We can think of total income being consumed (spent) or saved (or, equivalently, used to buy claims on assets). These savings can be used to buy investment goods (expenditure) and the market for these savings and investments clear at the 'natural rate' of interest.[6] Movements in interest rates will ensure that the expenditure is brought in line with production and income at some level where the factors of production are fully employed.

Keynes turned this observation inside out. In essence, he argued that it was not interest rates that adjusted to clear the market for savings – which we should think of as financial assets, with debt being financial liabilities – but income. This means that if there is an excess of savings, which are a function of aggregate income, then households will tend to reduce their consumption, which will drive down the level of overall income until savings equals investment. In this story it is not interest rates that are the final target of policy but the level of expenditure and income, or what came to be known as aggregate demand. Perhaps this is all very well known now. But it was a revolutionary insight in the interwar period.

---

[5] Diane Coyle has provided a nice history of GDP.
[6] See my work with Morris Perlman (2014) for more on the natural rate of interest.

Of course, we now also have been forcefully reminded that the flow of savings to investment can be disrupted in financial and economic crisis. And so behind the veil of even this classical scheme was an institution (or three) acting to maintain this flow in an orderly manner. We must not forget or underplay the importance of central banks in the classical scheme. The Bank of England, and other central banks, had adopted the role of helping to eliminate panics and ensure some ongoing financial stability. The development of tools to deal with crises was a long process, involving as much intuition as scientific analysis, but the orthodoxy was so underpinned. Walter Bagehot (1873) outlined his understanding of these principles in his description of the lender of resort function that central banks should adopt in a crisis:

(1) It should lend freely at a rate of interest relative to the pre-crisis interest rate that was high but only to borrowers with good collateral i.e. the kind of assets that the central bank would normally accept anyway;

(2) The valuation of these assets should be at some point between the pre-panic (high) price and the panic (low) price;

(3) Institutions with no good collateral cannot be lent to and they should be allowed to fail.

It is certainly possible to ascribe the regularity of banking crises in the United States in the late nineteenth and early twentieth centuries to the absence of a national central bank, the Federal Reserve System, until 1914. The powers of the Federal Reserve System were widened with the twin adoption of the Glass-Steagall Act in 1933 and the Banking Act of 1935, which introduced deposit insurance and separated commercial from investment banking.[7] It is also possible to argue that the classical system had at its heart a fragility not connected directly with Keynesian notions of insufficient demand but more a propensity to dislocate the transfer of savings to investment

---

[7] See Franklin Allen and Douglas Gale (2007) on this point.

because of financial crises. When these types of crises emerged it was not clear that interest rates were the correct tool to effect a recovery and neither was some direct stimulus to the economy but more a careful stewardship of the mechanism of financial transfer. But let us first turn to some facts.

2.2 THE INTERWAR FACTS

The period following World War I produced a temporary boom but a longer period of dislocation, called the Slump, which was much more substantive in the United Kingdom than the later more famous Depression. Despite the deflation induced by the need to return to the gold standard at the pre-suspension gold price, which implied an overvalued exchange at US $4.86, the economy was in a sustained recovery by 1922.[8] The Bank of England had a considerable degree of independence in the employment of Bank Rate and this was held lower than in other advanced countries. The deflation, which is a sustained fall in the general prices of goods and services, can be observed directly in the top left-hand panel of Figure 2.1 because the nominal index of GDP (which adds the actual quantity of production to that of the aggregate price level) is by 1930 some 20 per cent below the real index of the quantity of GDP, acted to increase the real value of nominal debt. As nominal debt represents under these circumstances a greater burden in terms of the overall price of goods and services, the payment of this higher level of real debt transfers more net wealth from debtors to creditors. But overall economic performance, in terms of aggregate income, was remarkably steady.[9] We can compare the progression of income in the United Kingdom with that of the leading industrial nation after WWI, the United States, and find that the start and end point of GDP in the interwar years looks very

---

[8] Donald Moggridge (1972) has produced the classic history of this policy decision.

[9] Do recall that this aggregate data was constructed mostly after WWII, so economic agents operating at the time could not have known with any degree of certainty the state of national income. Actually, month to month we are still walking through a series of doors into partially lit rooms.

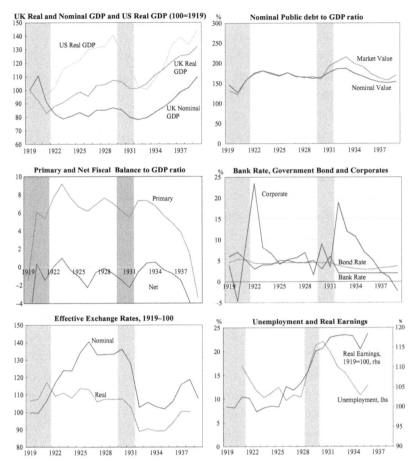

FIGURE 2.1 The interwar UK economy

much the same, but in the United States there was a substantially more volatile ride.

In fact, the fiscal position of the United Kingdom, as measured by the ratio of debt to GDP, acted as quite a constraint on the choices as to ongoing fiscal policy. It seems difficult to imagine, from a modern perspective, how much more loose fiscal policy could possibly have been in this period when public debt was already bumping along just under 200 per cent of national income. So even though average bond rates and the average yields on government debt were well under 5 per cent in this period, the sheer quantity of debt out-standing meant that a large primary surplus on government accounts of 6–8 per cent was eroded back to a slightly negative balance once interest payments had been accounted for; this helps understand better, it seems to me, the Treasury View.

Although Bank Rate and, correspondingly, the interest rate on government debt remained low, interest rates in the corporate bond market were volatile and sensitive to shocks, and we note that rates moved sharply up after the two post–WWI Cunliffe Committee reces-sions and persistently so in the 1930s, which may suggest that there were some supply disruptions limiting the availability of loanable funds. Consistent with this observation, we also note that there was a limited contribution from investment in both recoveries: both seem to more heavily dominated by consumption of the private and subse-quently public variety. Indeed, in an analysis of the lack of financial support for firms, the interwar Cunliffe Committee identified this is a problem that became known as the Macmillan Gap. The appreciation in the nominal exchange rate index in the period up to 1925 follows directly from the policy 'return to gold' at the pre-war exchange rate. The concurrent deflation meant that the real exchange rate – an index of the rate of exchange between home and overseas goods and ser-vices – was broadly stable, which may nevertheless still have been above the equilibrium exchange rate. It is a good example of apparent stability masking growing instability.

After a de facto suspension during the Great War, and eventu-ally a formal suspension of the gold standard in 1919, there was no concerted effort to seek a devaluation in the gold price of sterling. In fact, most efforts were driven towards seeking an early resumption of convertibility. There was considerable momentum for the return of the norm, as it was simply how it was done. The readoption of the gold standard at the pre-war rate has often been portrayed as an overvaluation at an unsustainable rate. And slowdown in subsequent economic performance would seem to add some weight to this obser-vation, as the overall price level continued to fall, albeit at a slower rate than prior to the readoption of gold. Narrow and broad money remained reasonably stable fractions of GDP but as the 1930–1931 recession took hold, both measures of the velocity of money circulation, which is the ratio of transactions to money holdings, fell markedly. Any real sign of dislocation was in the burgeoning unemployment rate, which had been at unacceptable levels of more than 10 per cent for most of the 1920s but then peaked at more than 20 per cent in 1931 in the middle of the second recession, over the same time that real wages had risen by nearly 20 per cent, which may not, if accurate, be consistent with a story about deficient demand. The immediate response involved cheap money, with Bank Rate cut to 2 per cent for the rest of the 1930s and it was only by around 1936 that government consumption played a major role in explaining output growth.

J. B. Priestly in *His English Journey* describes the interwar period, based on a journey in the autumn of 1934, brilliantly, as he describes the lasting impact on his hometown of Bradford (p.156):

> Not only have nearly all the big merchanting houses disappeared but a great many of the English firms too. Wool merchants, whose names seemed to us like the Bank of England, have vanished. Not one or two of them, but dozens of them. The great slump swept them away ... I am no economist, but it is obvious even to me this that this notion of there being a normal standard of trade is fallacious and dangerous. The situation is not merely changing temporarily all the time; it is changing for ever.

Rather than being a story of economic mismanagement and extreme dislocation, the interwar period looked more like an economy adjusting in various ways to an expensive war and its aftermath, trying to locate a stable anchor for money. Given the scale of the debt hangover and deflation, the post–WWI adjustment with primarily the classical tool of Bank Rate, unemployment apart, does not look like an unreasonable performance overall. And within the context of much of the fatalistic commentary, the United Kingdom actually benefitted from income some 30 per cent above its post-war level by the late 1930s. But the long view does tend to compress the impact of short-term vicissitudes and in some sense it is precisely that unknown but changing long run, reflecting the sifting nature of economic production to which Priestly alludes, that central banks are trying to understand when setting short-run policies.

2.3   OVER IN EUROPE

If the historical record on the interwar period is surprising, the famous four hyperinflations in Germany, Hungary, Austria and Poland in the early 1920s are less controversial to observers, as they had all been caused by the growth of unbacked fiat money issuance or what we now call the monetisation of debt.[10] The increase in the Hungarian price level is mirrored by the fall in the value of the Crown on the New York foreign exchange market. As is typical in the atypicality of hyperinflations, the collapse in value is quite astounding. The price index goes from 4,200 in July 1921 to over 2,000,000 by March 1924 and the Crown, which was worth 33 cents in July 1921, was worth less than 1 cent by July 1923. The hyperinflations were only solved when a form of co-ordination between monetary and fiscal regimes was adopted that implied the establishment of an independent central bank, which ran at arms' length from governments, with an obligation to sell debt to private or overseas individuals who would value the stock of debt in terms of the likely present value of the taxes that back the issuance, by which we mean that the debt repayments to the creditor will be actually be honoured by levying taxes in the future rather than there being a default of some sort.

We cannot be exactly sure what impact these hyperinflations had on the policymakers in the United Kingdom. But "Maynard Keynes wrote in 1924 that "it is common to speak as though, when a government pays its way by inflation, the people of the country avoid taxation. We have seen this is not so. What is raised by printing

---

[10] Tom Sargent (1982) tells the story very well.

notes is just as much taken from the public as is beer-duty or an income tax. What a government spends the public pays for. There is no such thing as an uncovered deficit. But in some countries it seems plausible to please and content the public, for a time being at least, by giving them, in return for the taxes they pay, finely engraved acknowledgements on watermarked paper. The income tax receipts, which we in England receive from the surveyor, we throw into the wastepaper basket: in Germany they call them banknotes and put them in their pocketbooks; in France they are called rentes and are locked up in the family safe". I take this observation to mean that any Treasury would have been quite wary of pushing expansionary fiscal policy, as it perhaps has always been and always will be. The need to capture resources and transfer them will always be limited to the need to nurture and respect the quantity of those resources. The Treasury recognises that it is no magician, unlike Montesquieu's (p. 73) mythical king:

> Moreover, the king is a great magician. He exerts authority even over the minds of his subjects; he makes them think what he wants. If there are only a million crowns in the exchequer, and he needs two million, all he has to do is to persuade them that one crown is worth two, and they believe it. If he is involved in a difficult war without any money, all he has to do is to get into their heads that a piece of paper will do for money, and they are immediately convinced of it.

2.4   THE POLICY ARENA

The dominant economic thinker at this time was, of course, Maynard Keynes. Although he wielded great influence over the Treasury and the Bank of England, the two revolutions he inspired in terms of economic theory and policy had not yet ran their course. Economic fluctuations were predominantly viewed as the revelation of nature rather than the obligation of government to attenuate. The one Treasury official who might be described as the main economist of note there after Keynes' exit in 1919 was Hawtrey, who felt that the trade cycle was mostly a monetary phenomenon and accordingly he was hugely influential, along with the governor of the Bank of England, in maintaining policies of cheap money.[11] The overriding objectives of policy seem to have been a fear of inflation, which was probably exacerbated by the continental experience, and consequent need to balance the budget. Without a clear theory of the aggregate relationship, which differs from that for a household, between prices, output and interest rates and without much of a statistical snapshot of the economy, it was very hard to formulate counter-cyclical policy. The first set of national accounts were not presented to the Treasury until 1941.[12]

Indeed, it appears that neither the exchange rate nor the budget were viewed as instruments of economic policy. Actually, the economy was mostly insulated from the worst impacts of the Great Depression by the fortunate accident of the gold standard exit, for which the Treasury seemed relieved and a member of the Labour government in 1931 famously said 'nobody told us we could do this'. Perhaps the ultimate expression of a change in the tack of policy towards output might be thought of as having been expressed in the publication of the *Employment Policy* White Paper of 1944, which stated that: the government accepts as one of their primary aims and responsibilities the maintenance of a high and stable level of employment after the war. Of course, in part such a commitment reflected the politics of mass unemployment before the war and the need to provide some comfort for those fearing a post-war slump of the type that had occurred after the Great War. But there was also a sense that the theoretical insights developed in the interwar period and harnessed during the war economy, alongside genuine statistical innovation, had perhaps led to a fundamental step forward in answering the

---

[11] I draw heavily here on the discussions in George Peden (1988) and Christopher Dow (1998).

[12] Peden, p. 42.

question of how to sustain the level of aggregate demand in an economy around its full employment level.

2.5   THE MULTIPLIER

That the astounding insight in this period now seems almost laughably obvious, reminds us how path-breaking insight can become conventional. In a static world there is a given level of income with some consumed and the rest saved to provide income in future periods. This can be thought of as a simple endowment economy, in which money simply facilitates intergenerational trade, as explained in the previous chapter. However, let us now suggest that the level of consumption continues to be a function of income but also that income is a function of the level of consumption. In this world, anything that induces a change in consumption may have persistent effects on the level of output. What modern economists now call, and indeed yearn for in their models, an amplification and persistence channel, was perhaps first articulated in the form of the multiplier. Allow me to explain.

Let us suppose that planned expenditure in terms of consumption, investment, government spending and net exports is related to the level of income (or supply) in an economy. But with each single unit increase in income, expenditure increases by something less than one unit because some fraction is saved. If planned income does not equal actual income, some adjustment will then take place because an equilibrium will imply that plans are fulfilled or revised! Clearly this economy will be in equilibrium when planned expenditure equals actual income.

Now let us consider an autonomous increase in expenditure, for example, from the pocket of a benign overseas oligarch – should such a person exist. This will act to raise the level of expenditure for every level of income. But it will also induce ultimately a higher level of income. This is because the higher level of overall expenditure produced by combined efforts of the domestic economy and the oligarch delivers more overall income into the hands of domestic consumers. Some fraction of this extra income will also be spent and this will act to raise overall income once again. This second increase in overall income will also lead

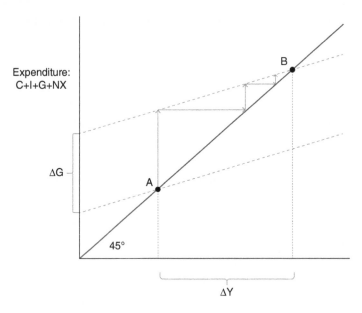

FIGURE 2.2 The multiplier mechanism

to a smaller increase in consumption and a further smaller increase in overall income. The process will continue until planned expenditure from this higher level of income equals the actual level of higher income. This process by which the final level of output is increased by more than the initial increase in expenditure is called the multiplier.

We may want to replace our notion of a benign oligarch with a democratic government that raises its consumption or lowers taxes, or even in terms of the 'animal spirits' of investors who rely on confidence to motivate their decisions. But any of these shocks may be able to set up a multiplier process. A question for any macroeconomist, and one which has not been adequately answered to this day is: what is the induced increase in the level of output from a given change in the government's fiscal position, that is what is the size of this multiplier? This is illustrated by Figure 2.2, where the ΔY (output) is greater than ΔG (government expenditure) as we move from the initial equilibrium of A to the final one of B. The answer will depend on whether the increase is considered temporary or permanent and on how households on average respond in terms of the split between consuming and saving. Thus, we need to know what happens to interest rates.

2.6 'MR KEYNES AND THE CLASSICS'

Now we can take the view that there is an impact from expenditure on final income; we can go on to solve for the final resting place, or equilibrium, level of output in terms of interest rates. Hicks (1937) suggested that we should interpret the many possible levels of output when the economy was under full capacity as points at which the goods market (for investment and saving) and the money market (for liquidity and money) both clear simultaneously. This analysis of the IS-LM schedules in a world of fixed prices has the advantage of involving a general equilibrium – an expression that simply implies a simultaneous analysis of all markets – for asset and goods markets, and of allowing us not only to think about the causes of output fluctuations in terms of these two schedules but to consider the efficacy of policies that alter the levels of expenditure or the stock of money, by also considering their impact on other markets.

The goods market can be considered to have cleared when savings equals investment, where the demand for and supply of goods is equal. And as income rises we may save a higher quantity of income, even if the savings rate is constant. This means that for the goods market to clear, at higher levels of income we need lower interest rates to induce a higher investment demand for the pool of savings at higher income levels so savings are so generated. We therefore can draw the equilibrium in the goods market as a downward sloping curve in interest rate-output space (R, Y in Figure 2.3) and the schedule can be shifted out (in) by autonomous increases (decreases) in the demand for goods.

In the money market, see the top left diagram in Figure 2.3, we shall assume that households hold the available stock of money for two reasons: a transaction and speculative, or asset purchase, motive. In the first instance, for reasons we have already discussed, households hold money in proportion to their expenditure, which is in turn linked to their income. In the second instance, they may hold money for the purchases of speculative assets and this speculative demand is inversely related to the interest rate. This is because the interest rate might be thought of as the cost of funding, the opportunity cost of purchasing assets or the discount factor on the expected returns from holding assets. With higher levels of income, the household will wish to hold more money for transactions, but if the quantity of money is fixed we need to substitute from speculative money holdings. This substitution can only be achieved if we increase the opportunity cost of holding speculative assets with higher interest rates. The equilibrium in the money market is therefore upward sloping and schedule can be shifted out (in) by increases (decreases) in the money stock, see top right diagram in Figure 2.3.

We are now in a position to consider the two sides of the interwar debate in IS-LM space.[13] Consider an LM schedule for which the demand for speculative money is very sensitive to changes in interest rates, so that the curve is rather flat, and an IS schedule for which the overall demand for goods is not very sensitive to changes in interest rates, so that the curve is rather steep. We can think of this position as broadly corresponding to the developing Keynesian attack on the existing orthodoxy. In this scenario, an increase in expenditure can increase output with little or no negative feedback from the effects of higher interest rates in the money market, and this takes us from point **b** to **c**. Even more so, any effects on interest rates can be offset by relatively small increases in the money stock, which would take us to point **d**. For schedules of this type, some form of fiscal policy that shifts out the IS curve may be particularly helpful in stimulating activity.[14]

The orthodox opposition to this view involves an inelastic demand for money and a spending schedule that is somewhat more

---

[13] With thanks to Roger Middleton, from whose excellent 1985 book I have learnt much.

[14] The middle row of Figure 2.3.

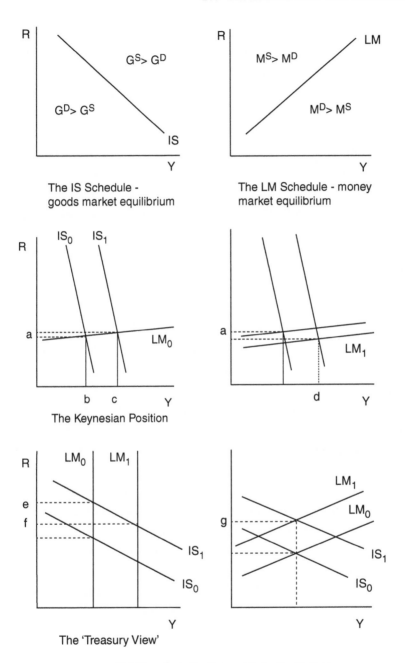

FIGURE 2.3 IS-LM analysis R = Interest Rate, Y = Output

sensitive to changes in interest rates. In this case, any attempt to use government spending will only tend to increase the prevailing interest rate, as any potential extra demand is simply 'crowded out' by higher interest rates at **e**. This can be offset to a degree by an autonomous shift in the money stock and induce higher demand for goods by reducing the interest rate to **f**. Indeed, under this scenario a negative movement in the LM schedule can induce quite a large fall in output, unless accompanied by a large autonomous shift out in goods demand. The dispute in policymaking is thus less about the actual mechanism or structure but more about which matters more quantitatively. In other words, it became an empirical question.

The broader picture is that this interpretation of the macroeconomic determination of output under fixed or sticky prices not only allowed us to consider the question of the multiplier accounting for any impact on interest rates but also to consider the efficacy of fiscal or monetary policy, as well as the extent to which outcomes might be co-ordinated or conflict with each other. The final panel on the bottom right-hand side illustrates such a conflict with loose fiscal policy being offset by tighter monetary policy at point **g,** leading to no change in output but higher interest rates. Indeed, one could imagine a reverse of this situation when we start at point **g** and offset looser monetary policy with tight fiscal policy again leading to no change in output, but a fall in interest rates. The basic story of output determined by demand, at least in the short run, with goods and asset markets clearing at any equilibrium point, is still the starting point for almost any macroeconomic analysis. These questions framed under IS-LM dominated post-war economic thinking and continue to provide the preliminary answers for which central banks return time and again. What is the interest rate that will clear the market for goods and that for money at a high level of employment.

2.7   SO WHAT DID HAPPEN?

Rather heroically and with the benefit of nearly a century of hindsight we might want to ask any number of questions based on this

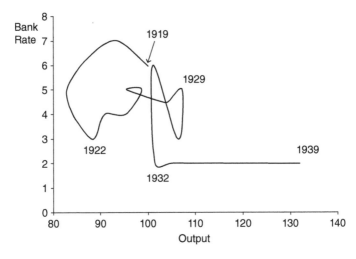

FIGURE 2.4 Output and interest rates, 1919–1939

IS-LM framework. In a series of famous debates, macroeconomists have continued to debate the extent to which the two interwar recessions might have been related to shifts in the IS or LM curves. The monetarist position is broadly one that argues that monetary policy was prematurely tightened and this drove interest rates up and output down; the proto-Keynesian view placed a greater weight on changes in expenditure in a demand deficient environment. Indeed it is questionable whether prices were even considered stable in this period, as the sustained deflation would according to Pigou, eventually have a wealth effect, as the real value of money balances would increase and cause the money curve to move out. We can plot the output level and Bank Rate from 1919 to 1939 in the same space as the IS-LM curve and imagine a large number of possible shapes and shifts that could explain the observed quantities and prices. For example, was the movement from 1932 to 1939 a successive increase in expenditure, or loose fiscal policy, against a flat LM curve? Or was it a combination of expansionary fiscal and monetary policy, with both curves shifting out? The art of identification is to place sufficient restrictions on these or other possibilities and emerge with one

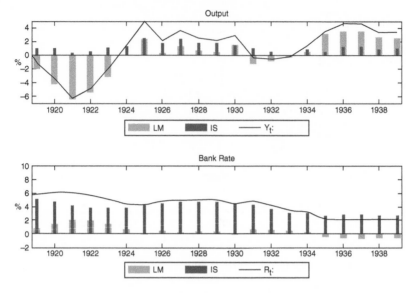

FIGURE 2.5 Decomposing output and Bank Rate, 1919–1939

answer, or at least the best answer or, then again, the least worst answer.

We can use modern techniques based on the impact of a shift in the IS curve on output and interest rates (they trace out the LM curve and move output and interest rates in the same direction) and the impact of an LM shift on output and interest rates (they trace out the IS curve and so move these output and interest rates in the opposite direction), to decompose movements in output and ascribe them to shifts in some measure to either of the curves. Essentially we generate many, many possibilities for the shifts and slopes of both curves and keep trying different ones, and then present the results of the most likely sequence: it is a trained guess.[15]

It would appear from the face value of this analysis that both post-war recessions were more obviously related to shifts in the LM schedule. We can see from the top panel of Figure 2.5 that it is the negative shifts in the identified LM curves that explain the deep

---

[15] Or what we now call Bayesian analysis.

recession of the early 1920s and the lighter one at the turn of the succeeding decade. If one were to believe this result, it would suggest that monetary policy instead of fiscal or expenditure was more to blame for the recessions, and perhaps a fiscal solution was not the way forward but rather, looser monetary policy. As you would expect from an economist, allow me to argue with these, my own, results.

There are a number of uncertainties in this estimate: (i) can we assume that the slopes of the schedules were the same throughout this exceptional period?; (ii) what if the data on output is measured with error or noise?; (iii) surely the high levels of unemployment must have meant that shifts in spending played an important role in explaining output growth; (iv) can we proxy economy-wide interest rates by Bank Rate alone?; (v) how do we deal with expectations of income and interest rates in this static framework?; and (vi) what about the possibility that changes in the aggregate price level may have induced shifts in output that are not well explored in this simple framework? These problems of identification and the relationship between policy and response plagues economics and particularly monetary policy judgements today, and certainly cause me to attach a large health warning of a pandemic-type size to these 'results'. The lags from output to inflation are long. But so are the lags before we can agree the historical record on what has actually happened in the past, even then we have to accept that for many economic policy issues we never will know exactly what happened and what is the cause of what we have observed. These identification problems mean that central bankers are constantly working with partial knowledge, and they know they are.

2.8   CONCLUDING REMARKS

The classical economy suggested that there was a unique market-clearing equilibrium, which swept up any fragments in the real side of the economy in terms of the demand for and supply of goods. The price level in this economy had no secular trend as the gold standard seemed to deliver long-run price stability, albeit at some cost in terms of year-to-year variance. The financial sector was insulated by high levels of liquidity and capital, and, in any case, the Bank of England and other national central banks had long adopted some form of Bagehot's principles in a crisis.

The shock of two recessions, exit from the gold standard – which had been an accidental fixture since 1717 – and ultimately the large and persistent levels of unemployment, convinced many that the classics needed to be recast. Keynes offered an answer. There was not necessarily a unique, full employment equilibrium and output was for the most part demand determined. This meant that something called macroeconomic policy might usefully be developed to manipulate demand through the money markets or goods markets to bring about a level of output consistent with full employment. In a world there the private sector seems to fall down on the job, the natural replacement is the state, which can marshal and collect information, well-meaning public officials and 'great minds' to help co-ordinate a better outcome for the macroeconomy. This change in tack was set in stone by the famous 1944 White Paper on Employment.

But if the state can help households and firms offset the negative impact of events, or what economists call shocks, it is not such a great intellectual leap for the state to take ultimate responsibility for economic stability. In a world that continues to be divided between monetarists and Keynesians, or progressive and conservative or expansionists and contractionists, we do need to remember that society has a choice, and perhaps a responsibility, to implement policies that influence demand. It is the evolution of that responsibility in the golden era we shall examine in the next chapter.

3   Fine-Tuning Out of Control

In which we travel from the certainties of picking a point on a trade-off between unemployment and inflation in order to engineer an acceptable outcome to the escalating frustrations that limit the scope for engineering. It turns out that expectations and learning make trade-offs unstable and may not be exploitable. It strengthened the hands of the conservatives rather than the activists, at least for a while.

This is what I mean when I say I would like to swim against the stream of time: I would like to erase the consequences of certain events and restore an initial condition. But every moment of my life brings with it an accumulation of new facts, and each of these new facts bring with it consequences; so the more I seek to return to the zero moment from which I set out, the further I move away from it.

Italo Calvino, *If on a Winter's Night a Traveller*, 1979

3.1   ENGINEERING STANDARDS

Monetary policy as we have seen started as a form of standardisation: 'this amount of paper is worth this much shiny metal and always will be' was the main linguistic directive of any monetary policymaker. Wider participation in the political decision-making process and a broader understanding of the problems caused by excessive business cycle volatility, particularly from the middle of the twentieth century, increased the onus on monetary policymaking to go further than merely setting standards. The move from a commodity currency to the fixed-but-adjustable exchange rate system of Bretton Woods, under which leading nations pegged their currency to the US dollar, may superficially not seem very important. Because, rather than fixing domestic currency value in terms of a block of shiny metal, it was now fixed in terms of some other reference currency, in this case the US dollar, which was itself fixed to the same shiny metal. However, a small advantage had been gained, we might say later that it was misused, but advantage there was; it was that the value of domestic currency could be changed relative to the reference currency and the domestic guardian of monetary standard could now also set the price of his or her currency externally to reflect and support adjustment to changing domestic conditions.

But did the standardiser have any practical or theoretical principles to guide him? An eternal trade-off remained, as the domestic guardian would neither want to become a debaser of the currency or the wearer of a monetary hairshirt. How could the guardian use his or her new powers wisely, particularly if the people or their elected representatives had asked for them, or expected them, to be unleashed?

3.2   THE ECONOMIST AS ENGINEER

How to put together the nuts and bolts of monetary policy can be hard to fathom when swimming in the opaque, muddy, waters of the economy. There are a number of elements to overcome. First, how exactly does setting a single short-term interest rate act to stabilise an economy that comprises so many households, firms, financial institutions, a substantial government sector and a host of (disinterested or even malign) overseas relationships? Secondly, there are a large number of institutional details to consider, such as the framework for monetary policy, the relationship between the Finance Ministry and the Central Bank and what might be the ultimate objectives of any stabilisation policy. Thirdly, the theory of monetary policy whilst first non-existent, quickly developed into a branch of 'control theory' and so became subject to severe technical barriers at the frontier. Finally, there is the aspect of the real data: how do we make decisions when the observed economy is not some clearly identifiable mass but a spongy construct based upon a myriad of observations or surveys announced on a daily basis? The mixture of institutional detail, high theory, data and, at times, low politics, can make monetary policy analysis a daunting mix for practitioner, instructor and student alike.

Metaphors can be useful when we are dealing with complex ideas and sometimes it can be a good idea, unlike drinks, to mix them. We tend to start with an analogy related to driving cars, steering ships or taking a shower in which, the policymaker is cast as the driver, pilot or bather. But, let us say, the pilot has severe informational problems, as he (or she) cannot know with a high degree of certainty where he is compared to where he would like to be. He also does not quite know how the machine will react when he asks it to help him get to where he would like to be. Finally, it may also be some time before he realises that he is or is not where he thinks he would like to be, and so he may frequently under- or even overshoot his final destination. Should your head be reeling, you will now be pleased to know that I am going to try ease you through these rather difficult kinds of control issues.

What we do in this chapter is tell the story of the evolution of thinking on monetary policy in the first few decades after World War II when the argument that the government was responsible for the short-term evolution of the economy had been won. So even though there were widespread controls on exchange rate movements under Bretton Woods, on capital controls and not a small degree of financial repression, monetary policy evolved into a control problem,[1] by which I mean a theory of policy that treated the economy as a system that could be manipulated using policy tools into behaving smack in line with policymakers' objectives, in the short run, in aggregate where inflation was low and growth was significantly positive and stable. If the economy could be so manipulated it would be said to be at its 'Bliss Point'. Actually, this kind of 'bliss' point proved rather hard to engineer, as a number of increasingly problematic trade-offs emerged between output and inflation that effected a change of plan. So from a simple control problem of a known system with well-understood tools, monetary policy subsequently evolved into a game concerned with the interplay between smart agents, not so smart agents, central banks with imperfect information, and governments

---

[1] We might think of capital controls as limits on the quantity and type of funds that can flow from one country to another and financial repression as domestic policy that limits interest rates from rising to levels that will clear markets.

determined to stay in power. But let us first look at the most basic of trade-offs between inflation and output, the Phillips curve.

3.3   STABILISATION POLICY

The technical steps in defining a monetary policy problem were spelt out in the immediate post-war period. The case for directing the economy resulted from two distinct parables. One, the enduring memory of interwar economic failures and two, the positive experiences of a running a war economy contributed much. Ultimately it was a posthumous and durable triumph for Maynard Keynes, so much so that direct responsibility for the growth rate in a market economy still seems to lie with the government. This has frequently set up a difficult dynamic under which the government can be prone to applying pressure to the central bank for lower interest rates. Central bankers learnt that it did not help the efficacy of policy if they seemed in thrall to politicians, whatever may be the truth of the situation.

Once people turned to the question of how to set and think about policy in real time, it was clear that a number of gaps in our knowledge existed. Many ideas seeped in from engineering with, perhaps most famously, Bill Phillips' (a hydraulic engineer with an economics bent) observation of a trade-off between spare capacity and inflationary pressure. The Phillips curve, as it still known, tells the policymaker the likely current rate of exchange if we want to engineer a little more (less) unemployment and a little less (more) inflationary pressure. In effect, the curve offers a menu of alternatives that the policymaker may wish to set against his current preferences for output and inflation. It is such a crucial question for policymakers and theoreticians that the curve itself has gone through many permutations, as the profession has tried to understand shifts or breakdowns in seemingly stable relationships.

The original Phillips paper, published in 1958, traced a negative relationship between the rate of change of money wages and unemployment from 1861 to 1913 (in the United Kingdom and shown

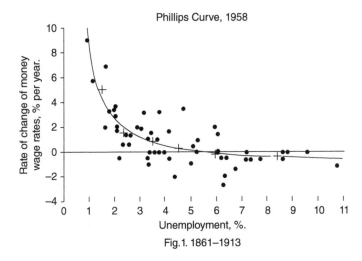

FIGURE 3.1 From Phillips' paper in *Economica* (1958)

in Figure 3.1) and offered a statistical observation, rather than a theory, that was tested against subsequent observations over two sub-periods from 1913 to 1948 and then from 1948 to 1957. To some degree it allowed both proponents of importance of a demand-led inflation and a cost-push inflation to make their cases, where the former argues that inflation tends to result from excessive growth in spending and the latter that it results from escalating prices of inputs in the production process. But it was the seeming robustness of the relationship in other countries that was persuasive, and so the ideas were developed at length by American economists Paul Samuelson and Bob Solow into a specific menu of trade-offs between inflation and output, rather than money wages and unemployment. The basic idea was simply that increasing levels of capacity utilisation in aggregate were likely to be associated with greater upwards pressure on wages and prices and, I add a sub-clause, at *an increasing rate*, as resources became more scarce their prices would tend to rise more quickly. The observation was also reasonably symmetric as reducing levels of capacity utilisation were likely to be associated with greater downward pressure on wages and prices.

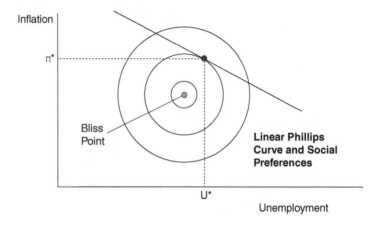

FIGURE 3.2 The policy problem with trade-off

We can now combine two ideas to give us the options facing a monetary policymaker, which are illustrated in Figure 3.2. The ideal level of inflation and output, which we can think of as simply a negative function of unemployment, can be thought of as the joint targets for the central banker. These targets may be imposed by the government on some type of ad hoc basis but, if democracy is working, may also represent social preferences; these may not necessarily be fixed for all time. If we place the same weight on any deviation of inflation or unemployment from this target – and recall that all the points on a circle are the same distance from the centre – then we quickly realise that the performance of the economy can be measured or valued by which concentric circle the inflation and unemployment levels sit. The nearer we are to the Bliss Point, the better. If we then approximate the non-linear Phillips curve by a straight line so that the rate of exchange between inflation and unemployment is constant, we can then see that the best performance the central bank can achieve is the point that corresponds to [π*] and [U*]. Even if the inflation target was lower or there was a desire for lower unemployment, both could not be achieved because of Phillips constraint that says the economy has to lie on the line and if one objective were pursued, society would be worse off because we would always be further form the Bliss Point. We might also think of the level of unemployment at this level as its natural rate (NRU), that is, the one consistent with low and stable growth as workers spend some time looking for work and the process of firm death and birth throws some unemployment into the economy.

However, in the 1960s, inflation seemed to become increasingly unhinged from the level of unemployment, or more generally spare capacity. This led to the development of the idea of a so-called accelerationist Phillips curve, that posited a relationship between the rate of change in inflation and the output gap,[2] which meant simply that the level of inflation itself was independent of the state of spare capacity and any shifts in capacity constraints will tend to alter permanently the inflation rate in one direction or the other. This reformulation of the Phillips curve allowed any given level of output to be associated with any given level of inflation and this seemed to help people understand why inflation had become so sticky when it had ratcheted up. It also implied that getting inflation down from a high level might require several bouts of lower demand, which ultimately became known as disinflationary paths and by less generously minded people as recessions.

As economists then tried to think about the implications of rationality and the use of information, an interest in the formation of expectations for future wage and price setting started to take a serious hold. A simple thought experiment will explain why: if you are setting production levels today and you know that prices or wages are likely to be high tomorrow, as opposed to yesterday when prices and wages were low, should you not build these higher prices and wages rather than yesterday's lower prices into your plans? If you do not respond to these expectations you may lose a certain fraction of the value of your sales, depending on much extra demand for your product results at these lower prices and, more importantly, you will

---

[2] So rather than controlling the first derivative of the price level, inflation, we then became interested in the second derivative, or the rate at which inflation changed.

not have sufficient cash flow to buy the next round of inputs at these elevated prices. So you will tend to raise your prices along with your expectations.

Once output has been set in line with expected inflation, it would change from the level that had been planned only if prices and wages differed substantially from those expectations, and only as long as it took for producers and wage setters to learn the new likely level of inflation. It was then not such a large leap to locate what became known as the expectations-augmented Phillips curve. This idea was championed by Milton Friedman famously in his 1968 AEA address, where he told us that inflation had to surprise us in order to effect some change in labour supply, and hence, output, but that this effect was strictly temporary as households and firms would quickly come to accept and plan around this new inflation rate. In the language that was used at the time, there was a level of unemployment *qua* output at which inflation would not change or accelerate, and this became known rather unattractively but quite literally as the non-accelerating inflation rate of unemployment, NAIRU.

Let us start from our original equilibrium in Figure 3.3 and imagine that the central bank springs an inflation that takes the

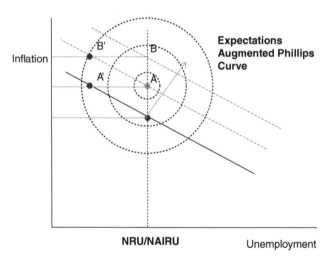

FIGURE 3.3 Expectations shifting the Phillips curve

economy to [A']; this will temporarily reduce real wages and lower unemployment, but once firms, workers and households expect this higher inflation rate, the trade-off will have to encompass this higher level of inflation for all levels of unemployment and hence the Phillips curve will shift out taking us to [A]. So even if we return to the neighbourhood of the NAIRU, inflation will have ratcheted up. Should a policymaker repeat the medicine, the economy will then end up at [B], via a step through [B']. Finally, note that because inflation is now higher, the economics of the trade-off mean that the policymaker would prefer slightly higher unemployment and slightly less inflation if possible or politically acceptable, as that would minimise the distance to the Bliss Point. I have drawn this as a thick path for a long-run trade-off that is actually positive! Not only does trying to exploit the Phillips curve to reduce unemployment not have any permanent impact on anything other than inflation, it may set up a disruptive game between the monetary policymaker and workers, where the former prefers a little more unemployment and a little less inflation and the latter prefers the converse. I think it might well be a very helpful parable to help us think about the struggles many of us observed in the 1970s and 1980s.

The key point here is that we had moved decisively away from price pressures emerging from a given level of output, which could thus be controlled relatively simply with reference to output, but to a world in which it was expectations of inflation that acted as an additional constraint, if not the overriding determinant of outcomes, on the ability of policymakers to deliver any given level of inflation. To this day, the role of expectations remains key to understanding macroeconomic models. Bob Lucas and Lionel Rapping went further in the late 1960s and early 1970s and suggested that it was only inflation 'surprises', as they became known, relative to rationally formed expectations, that would induce unplanned levels of aggregate output. The unplanned disruption in output would thus only last as long as the surprise, just as a surprisingly empty or congested road will tend to induce deviations in the actual time of arrival at one's destination for dinner compared to the expected time of arrival. It is not going to alter the overall supply of food or the time it takes to prepare it. The imperative to surprise had profound implications for the operation of monetary policy, as it motivated a process blanketed in stealth, so as to operate by shock – more on this later – which by its nature implied quite forcefully that it had strictly short-lived effects.

Whether a Phillips curve in terms of employment or a (Bob) Lucas surprise (aggregate) supply curve, the introduction of expectations into the framework was not only long overdue but also an explicit recognition that economist-engineers had to deal with a dynamic system that would itself both learn and be difficult to fool – a point to which we shall also return. The Phillips curve has had as many incarnations, in the manner of some of the more familiar ancient gods, to the extent that if you want to know something about an economist's views about the importance of stabilisation policy, ask her in what kind of Phillips curve do they believe. The most recent incarnation is the so-called New Keynesian Phillips curve, which relates the current level of the output gap or (economy-wide marginal costs) to a point on the trade-off between inflation today and tomorrow. Some will plump for a purely forward-looking Phillips curve, some will prefer a backward-looking curve and some will prefer a hybrid which combines the two. I have also had conversations with many prominent central bankers who deny that any such thing actually exists and certainly that any empirical estimates of any trade-off should not be used to inform monetary policy.[3]

3.4   CAN YOU GO BACKWARDS AND FORWARDS AT THE SAME TIME?

The trade-off of choice will tell you much about any particular economist's views about how policy works. Let us imagine a policymaker called Schulze who believes only in a forward-looking Phillips curve.

---

[3] Roger Farmer is very clear on this point in his published works.

It turns out that this belief is actually shorthand for inflation that can only be stabilised by controlling our expectations of the current and future stream of output gaps.[4] In Schulze's world it is the expected path of future policy rates that is the key to determining the extent to which any shock to demand or costs that may come along will impact on inflation today because plans for future output will depend on the expected responses of policymakers. So let us suppose that there is an unanticipated increase in expenditure today and/or something nasty expected tomorrow; this would not necessarily be inflationary if the policymaker pre-emptively raised interest rates by just enough to offset the present value of this shock. Actually, it is quite self-serving because if such a sequence of events turned out to be perfectly true and the central bank had offset a shock perfectly, we mortals would not even see the shock.

Alternatively, policymaker Chatelain might believe in a backward-looking Phillips curve, in which inflation responds only to past output gaps, and so really thinks that inflation can only be controlled in the future by altering the actual path of output. In this world we get to see an increase in expenditure today, but we wait until tomorrow before we do anything because we need to see that output and inflation have risen before acting. Of course when we act, inflation only falls after we bring output down, so in this system there are lags galore, as output accelerates followed by inflation, with policymakers slowly rousing themselves to bear down on output with inflation returning eventually to target. When comparing the two in the presence of high output and inflation today, what will these two people advise? Schulze will argue for plans to be announced about the need for tighter policy so that in expectation, output will be lower and this will actually lower inflation now in his world. Chatelain, though, wants more tangible evidence of the effects of policy before he acts.

---

[4] Many economists use the phrase marginal costs rather than the output gap; the former is simply the wage rate divided by the marginal product of labour and proportional to measures of unit labour costs.

Table 3.1. *Confronting views and outcomes*

	Belief	Confronting Phillips Curve Views and Outcomes	Forwards	Backwards	Hybrid	Mean	St. Dev.
			Rank	Rank	Rank		
Schulze	Forwards		1	3	2	2	1
Chatelain	Back		3	1	2	2	1
Clegg	Hybrid		2	2	1	1.7	0.6

He wants to see higher interest rates bring down output in reality so that agents in the midst of a recession dare not seek inflationary wage rises or mark-ups, and thus deflation has to be engineered by a painful operation. One might imagine that Schulze is an activist who always calls for interest rate action plans in response to economic news so that exuberant expectations can be tempered, whereas Chatelain may be a more considered type of policymaker because he thinks that actual output has to change to bring about changes in inflation, and this mean the loss of jobs and livelihoods.

There may even by a third hybrid type of person, let's call her Clegg, who may accept both the case for expectations-led inflation but also some possibility that agents may need recession or booms to nudge their own learning about the state of the economy. Although seemingly mixed up, Clegg actually occupies the high ground because to the extent that we do not know and probably cannot know whether Schulze or Chatelain are right, Clegg gives us an answer that will be least bad in the event of either Schulze or Chatelain winning the policy argument by force of character but while getting the facts wrong. Table 3.1 illustrates that alongside the beliefs, we look at whether the world is backward-looking, forward-looking or a hybrid: Schulze has a forward belief; Chatelain a backward; and Clegg a hybrid. The table shows the rank of each belief in comparison to the world we actually may have in terms of each of the three possibilities.

The final two columns show the average rank and the standard deviation of that rank across the evenly possible outcomes. Even though the hybrid will not dominate if we know for certain which version of the Phillips curve is 'truth', if we do not know which one and perhaps this may even change from time to time, it makes a lot of sense to be a hybrid thinker because we do better on average and have the least variance in rank-ordered outcomes. One thing to remember in economics is that convex combinations tend to be a good hand versus even a straight flush in a repeated game.

The Phillips curve is more that just a menu; at a general level it represents a metaphor for the structure of the economy as we understand it. Phillips himself created a number of machines that showed the circulation of demand through an economy and corresponded closely to the workings of a system of water pumps, from which a generation of post-war economists learnt that it was possible to think at some sectoral level, but also that these sectors added up to an aggregate flow of expenditures that would determine national income. The Phillips curve really is just a statement of some economic structure that traces the impacts of shocks to output or inflation in the short run, and so when we consider the theory of economic policy, we perhaps ought to move on to consider the role of structure in determining optimal choice.

3.5 TINBERGEN-THEIL

The apogee of the first scientific approach to monetary policymaking was the development of the Tinbergen-Theil framework, developed by Dutch economists Jan Tinbergen and Henri Theil. This approach had three ingredients: the preferences of society and hence the policymaker over inflation and output growth; the structure of the economy – typically an estimated trade-off (Phillips curve) between inflation and output; and the policy instrument or rule. The basic idea was simple, decide social preferences towards inflation and/or output; estimate the relationship in aggregate between output and inflation; and work out the appropriate level for policy rates or more accurately the typical way in which policy would respond to evolutions in the economy, which we might call *a feedback rule*. With sufficient clarity on preferences, structure and instrument choice, even an *optimal* feedback rule could be written down and, in principle, followed.

From the considerable and helpful perspective of time, it seems to me that post-war optimism about building a better future through empirical observation and engineered calculation had clearly infected monetary policymaking. Another good and parallel example was the development of high-rise concrete blocks; we discovered that, although the views were often remarkable, the lack of personal and public space led to a deterioration in the quality of life (and arguably mutual respect within communities) and also may have involved the creation of unstable structures. The dangers of over-engineered monetary policy were actually not that dissimilar; rather than leading to more economic stability, the search for an optimal policy rule may have led to more instability as 'fine-tuning' demand to match supply might have asked too much of uncertain data and unstable economic structures.

The problems of over-engineering, as we shall discover, do not mean we do not try to engineer better outcomes, as no economist is working as a direct descendent of Voltaire's Dr Pangloss:

> 'It is demonstrable', said he, 'that things cannot be otherwise than as they are; for all being created for an end, all is necessarily for the best end. Observe, that the nose has been formed to bear spectacles—thus we have spectacles. Legs are visibly designed for stockings—and we have stockings. Stones were made to be hewn, and to construct castles—therefore my lord has a magnificent castle; for the greatest baron in the province ought to be the best lodged. Pigs were made to be eaten—therefore we eat pork all the year round. Consequently they who assert that all is well have said a foolish thing, they should have said all is for the best'.

We want to improve on what we see. So the post-war argument proceeded in the following manner. In order to locate an optimal policy is was necessary to choose an economic structure that was thought to be stable and that was sufficiently close enough to the behaviour of the actual so that it might be called accurate. For this we needed a set of behavioural relationships between the components of aggregate demand and the factors that explained their behaviour, or what some economists call drivers. As Ragnar Frisch put it in his Nobel Prize lecture, delivered alongside that of Tinbergen in 1970: 'The English mathematician and economist Stanley Jevons (1835–1882) dreamed of the day when we would be able to quantify at least some of the laws and regularities of economics. Today – since the break-through of econometrics – this is not a dream anymore but a reality.'[5] With no wish to denigrate Ragnar Frisch, it is surprising how similar this statement sounds to those of central bankers in the first decade of this century who had started to take much of the credit for an apparent reduction in macroeconomic volatility. As ever, nemesis lays in wait for hubris. We typically seem to be most confident just before a crisis hits. The timelessness of this observation is as true in 2020 as it was in 2007 and 1989.

Let us not go too far, too quickly, though, because some of the contributions have proved durable. The Tinbergen-Theil framework allowed us to consider questions such as the number of degrees of freedom available for policymakers. By this I mean that with one independent instrument of policymaking it was only possible to sta-bilise fully one argument in the preference function, that is inflation or output. Typically, if we only had the short-term policy rate under our control we would have to decide on whether it was inflation or output that we wanted to stabilise in the face of stochastic shocks.[6] This axiom became known as the Tinbergen counting principle: that we could target as many variables as we had independent instruments of monetary policy. Figure 3.4 illustrates the Bliss Point, now in terms

---

[5] From *Utopian Theory to Practical Applications: The Case of Econometrics*, 1970, p. 12.

[6] A stochastic process is drawn from a known or given random probability distribution or pattern but any one draw, or shock, cannot be predicted precisely.

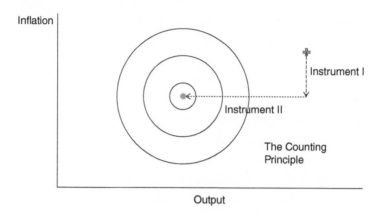

FIGURE 3.4 Counting instruments and objectives

of output, rather than unemployment, and inflation that for any starting point, [✦], if we have two independent instruments, the first of which can reduce inflation with no impact on output and the second, which can reduce output without effecting inflation, we can always recover the Bliss Point. But it is hard to think of a tool that cannot affect inflation and not output and vice versa, and so the principle further implied that if there were more objectives than available policy instruments, then we would have to accept a trade-off between the objectives; that is, choose some point that did not meet both objectives fully but only each in some limited degree.

The analysis of the question of policy trade-offs can be viewed as a direct descendent of the idea of the Phillips curve in the first place; that is, having observed some tendency for inflation and output (or capacity) to offset each other, we can choose to exploit this trade-off systematically in terms of the level of output or inflation we might expect to see given a shock and our best guess of the impact of any policy action. However, if we are to accept that we have little impact on the long-run rate of output, we might with considerably less authority (to control the economy) simply accept that in trying to stabilise the economy there will be some variance in inflation and output around their long-run trend and the choice is really about

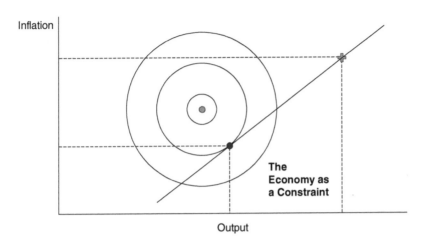

FIGURE 3.5 The economy as a constraint

minimising these variances, subject to some deep preferences about whether, as a society, we dislike inflation or output variance more. Again, with only one independent policy instrument available it is possible to categorise different policy responses (or rules) in terms of the resultant inflation–output variance frontier.[7] Either way, in terms of levels or variances, accepting that social welfare is some function of both inflation and output, as with most choices, we will have to accept some trade-off. While I have concentrated on the trade-off between two aggregate measures of activity, output and inflation, trade-offs might also appear in the policy choices between different types of households and between different sectors. A classic trade-off involves the expectation that the banking sector can support an economy in recession by taking on risk but at the cost to its future capacity to lend into a recovery.

The debate on monetary policy then shifted from the implications of any given instrument or set of instruments for the available set of choices to an analysis of the correct instrument itself. Let us go back to the equilibrium in the goods and asset markets determined by

[7] See Fuhrer (1997).

IS-LM analysis and suppose that the market for money clears at a given quantity and interest rate. Let us further assume that the current quantity of money is consistent with a level of aggregate demand that also meets price stability. So the policy rate, determined in the cleared money market, will then also be consistent with an acceptable degree of macroeconomic stability. Let us now consider some perturbations, *aka* shocks, in the money market, that lead to temporary changes in the market-clearing level of policy rates and will lead to temporary deviations in the policy rate from this initial, what might be termed natural, level and act to alter aggregate demand. What should be done?

The key question is the extent to which shocks emanating from the money market can or should be stabilised by setting interest rates directly, or indeed whether an alternative method may be required, for example, controlling the money stock directly. In the seminal analysis of this question, Bill Poole (1970) analysed the impact on the variance of output from either setting interest rates and letting money find its level, or controlling the quantity of the money supply and allowing interest rates to find their level – because we cannot set both money supply and interest rates. The basic answer is to choose the instrument that leads to the least variance in the output objective; so if we first fix interest rates and changes in money demand lead to considerable output volatility, it might be better to try and control the quantity of money and let interest rates move, or conversely, if we first try and fix money supply but find that interest rates are very sensitive to changes in the demand for money and hence output starts to become volatile, we might prefer to move back to choosing the interest rate.

The left-hand panel of Figure 3.6 illustrates two possible LM curves. The flatter one, LM2, implies a fixed interest rate and no control over money and the steeper LM1 line implies that interest rates will be allowed to rise to choke off excessive demand for money at higher levels of equilibrium in the goods market. In this economy, if all we are interested in is the variance of output and if the shocks

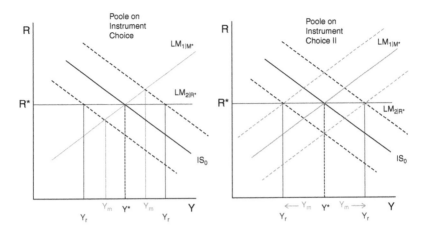

FIGURE 3.6 Poole's problem: Fixing money or interest rates

we observe are all confined to the spending equation, then by allowing interest rates to change we will engineer a lower variance of output, albeit at a cost of a higher variance in the interest rate instrument. We can see that the range of variation in Y_m is less than the range under Y_r.

A simple analogy here is found from my limited experience at the gym. If we want to loose 300 calories, we can set the time we spend on the treadmill and let the speed be determined by the need to loose 300 calories. On the other hand, we can set the speed and let the time flow until we have lost the 300 calories. If we set both time and speed, we cannot – unless by accident – be sure that we have lost 300 calories more or less, and then we have to choose one or the other and we would choose the one that results most likely in 300 calories being lost.[8] If we introduce an element of uncertainty, by which I mean that given that we may be determined to lose 300 calories at the gym but may not be able to rely on the speedometer, we might be better off fixing our time, or if we cannot rely on our clock, we might

[8] A keen amateur photographer might talk about aperture priority or shutter priority for evaluating correct exposures, but younger readers may not have a clue about what that means.

better off fixing our speed; the choice thus depends on the quality of the instruments, as well as the fact that we simply want to lose 300 calories. So if our instruments are faulty or noisy, we may not want to rely on one alone.

Poole thus also showed that, in general, neither method would necessarily stabilise the economy better than the other, as it depended on the relative magnitude of shocks in the money market or the interest rate–sensitive sectors, as well as the sensitivity of output to these respective shocks. And, of course, shocks and sensitivities are parameters to be estimated and thus subject to considerable measurement uncertainty. The right-hand panel of Figure 3.6 goes on to show that if we choose to allow interest rate to move, but there are shifts in the asset market equilibrium, which may result from any change in the demand for speculative assets from confidence or risk, we then can even become indifferent between the two alternatives.

An often overlooked implication of this analysis was that in general, some partial use of both instruments – looking at the clock and monitoring speed but not being bound to both – was likely to stabilise the output better than one instrument alone, a point to which we shall return, but one that is perhaps echoed by the recent experience of policymakers worldwide, as they have had to augment interest rate tools with direct expansion of the central bank balance sheet, or the issuance of monetary liabilities. In other words, we are back to some convex combination and this axiom becomes problematic for the policymaker, even with one independent instrument, as how we decide to control its level may matter quite a lot. It gets knotty very quickly. Indeed, how we operate in the money markets to bring about market clearing at an acceptable level of both money and interest rates may itself be subject to much vacillation in monetary practices.

To some extent, Robert Mundell gave us the end point of this type of reasoning. The Tinbergen-Theil framework helps us think about, within a simple economic structure, what kind of policy with what kind of instrument might bring about the best outcomes. To this

Mundell made two contributions. First, let us imagine we have two independent instruments, let us call them monetary and fiscal policy. Let us suppose we have two objectives, inflation and output. Should we use a combination of both instruments to hit some combination of both targets – the nuclear parenting option with two parents and two children? Or ought we to assign one instrument to one target, like one parent to each child? The monetary policy answer is, in general, the latter, as we might have an idea of which instrument (or parent) might do best with each objective and so, typically, assign monetary policy to inflation and fiscal policy to output stabilisation. A broad classification that still has much support across the profession. Of course, it is more complicated than that, as we shall later learn, because neither monetary nor fiscal policy nor output and inflation are strictly independent of each other.

His second contribution was to ask when two or more economies should decide to use the same policy instrument; the answer was when their respective economies suffer (or benefit) from similar synchronised aggregate demand shocks. For this contribution he was awarded the Nobel Prize in 1999, exactly thirty years after Jan Tinbergen. And Mundell's answer inverts the earlier reasoning. Remember, we need many independent instruments to meet many independent objectives, but we might only need one instrument if the objectives, to an acceptable level of comprise, are not independent. That argument will go through for inflation and output as much as it might for a set of economies considering monetary union. In this sense, Mundell simply pointed out that if economies were highly synchronised, then they may not lose very much in social welfare terms, from having a single interest rate across the countries, set centrally. As early as 1961 James Meade thought European economies were not sufficiently well synchronised and in his famous paper on optimal currency areas Mundell writes that 'Meade ... argues that the conditions for a common currency in Western Europe do not exist, and that, especially because of the lack of labor mobility, a system of flexible exchange rates would be more effective in promoting balance-of-payments equilibrium and internal stability.' Both Meade and Mundell won Nobel Prizes but it seems to me that Meade also understood the propensity for international payment problems rather well.

This point about sufficient synchronisation was pursued and investigated to an absurd degree by many analysts as they tried to answer Mundell's question with empirical investigation in the run-up to the creation of European Economic and Monetary Union.[9] It was found that many further questions needed to be answered. Let me list a few. What matters is not whether all the exogenous shocks were common but whether they arose from the kind of demand shocks that monetary policy was good at stabilising through interest rates. If they arose from other kinds of sources, for example, productivity or fiscal policy or indeed monetary policy itself, then this aspect of any synchronisation or not was essentially irrelevant. As well as the overriding source of shocks being spending shocks, it was therefore necessary to establish whether the primitive shocks, particularly real shocks, were strongly correlated across the EU countries – to the extent that we might then treat the independent states as one state. The unanswered question was then, how correlated was sufficiently correlated? Finally, we might also find that even if shocks are of the type that can be stabilised and are sufficiently correlated, we want to know that the response to a monetary policy action would be similar across these states, so that we would not be creating divergence by adopting the same interest rates. The empirical case could not I think be made one way or the other, which strikes as something of a failure of economic science.

As we drill deeper into the implications of any guiding principle for setting monetary policy, we find that its application tends to be a little more difficult than the rhetorical echo of an original paper, or insight, might imply. We find a train of thought that moves us radically away from the calculation of optimal operating procedures and

---

[9] I must point to my own culpability here!

towards very simple policy prescriptions, or what might be called heuristics. Conversations and judgments, even food and wine, are the typical precursors to decision-making and often require a light touch on principles and a heavier weight on context and feasibility.

3.6   THE LIMITS OF OUR KNOWLEDGE

The engineering solution that the Tinbergen-Theil framework hankered after was, I think, a subject of distaste for many: it asked too much of our state of knowledge and, in particular, of our ability to measure accurately the state of the economy and our likely impact on it as policymakers. That is not to say that the policy stabilisation problem was therefore one from which we ought to walk away as economists. But one that should have at its heart a considerable degree of circumspection: *cura te ipsum* as one might say to a physician.

A Popperian challenge was issued early on in this process. How can we construct monetary policy subject to the poor state of attainable knowledge for our heroic social engineers? Milton Friedman (1958), in his *Program for Monetary Stability*, made an astounding yet incredibly simple point; if we imagine the economy moving from year to year it will have a defined variance, some movement around its mean. For example, output may grow at 2 per cent on average per year but it may be known to vary around 2 per cent on either side of this mean some 95 per cent of the time. The mean and variance of output growth in the absence of any policy action is then known as defined; let us call this exogenous output growth. Now if we apply some policy function to that rate of economic growth, economic growth will consequently take on the characteristics of both the exogenous rate of output growth and the impact on output from the policy instrument. Output, as we observe it, will thus be the property of a joint function, that of exogenous output plus the response of output with respect to any policy.

Output, after the policy intervention, may thus tend to have a higher variance, as it will incorporate the variance of exogenous output and the variance induced by policy. Output growth may then actually become *more* uncertain, that is, with a *higher* variance than before unless we can be pretty sure that the impact of policy on exogenous output growth is significantly stabilising. In practice this means that exogenous output growth moves negatively, and consistently, with the growth in output induced by the policy; that is, we have to be sure that despite the observation, execution and transmission lags of policy and our uncertainty about policy multipliers, that when we cut interest rates, output will rise in time to offset a recession, and when we raise them output will fall in time to prevent a boom. A moment's thought will make us think about all the difficulties that this kind of negative or counter-cyclical policy has to overcome. As much as any other insight based on his work with Anna Schwartz, published in 1963 on the importance of maintaining medium-term growth in money in line with the growth in planned nominal expenditures, this little warning about the danger of stirring up more rather than less volatility when using monetary policy, has always stayed clearest in my mind and that of other policy-oriented economists, It remains a money minder maxim.

Bill Brainard (1967) took this idea about how to minimise the variance of the objective variable further in an important way. From the Tinbergen-Theil perspective, one instrument could be used to stabilise one objective. But then given uncertainty in outcomes, it became an issue of probability as to whether an instrument of policy can be manipulated in such a manner to bring about the preferred stabilising rather than destabilising outcome. However, what if in a manner similar to Milton Friedman's policymaker, we do not know the precise impact of a given change in the policy instrument on the objective? It is one thing to try and identify the shock and work out what the best response is, but it is quite another if the response itself induces even more uncertainty in expected outcomes. This becomes particularly problematic with policy acts with a lag. In Brainard's case the insight is that because any estimated response of the target variable to a change in the policy instrument is subject to considerable

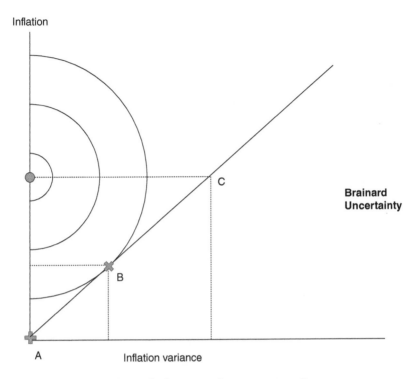

Inflation

Brainard
Uncertainty

Inflation variance

FIGURE 3.7 The gradualist approach to monetary policy

uncertainty, if we try to close the gap between the current value of the objective and our target for that objective, the only definite outcome is that we will be injecting some expected variances into the policy objective.

This insight introduced another trade-off. Figure 3.7 shows this trade-off as increases in variance of inflation for every unit increase in inflation. So if we were to start at [A] it is not optimal to hit the inflation target at [C] because here the level of inflation variance means that we are further away from Bliss Point than if we choose to move inflation only to [B]. Even if on average you can calculate the response to close the gap between where you want inflation to be and where it currently is, because that very action is costly in terms of the expected variance of inflation, you would be better off, as would society, if you chose to do a little less; that is, the policymaker will be willing to trade-off a small miss in the inflation target for a little less expected increase in variance. At a stroke, the fine-tuner's ability to control outcomes was, once again, undermined. It was not only that ill-timed monetary policy may end up stoking rather than attenuating the business cycle, it turned out that the policymaker ought to restrict him or herself to baby steps when stabilising the economy, because it could never be known what impact a given change in rates, or some other policy instrument, might have on the economy. A new term entered the language of monetary policymakers, who as well as dealing with additive or exogenous shocks, also now had to consider the probability that their own actions, when interacting with the economy, were likely to lead to multiplicative uncertainty and the response was a gradualist, or conservative central banker. The gradualist central banker might go for the same destination as the one who has full knowledge, or thinks she does, but aim to arrive slowly in baby steps. The conservative central banker is always aiming to do less than the full information alternative. The gradualist central banker might stop overnight three times on her way to John O'Groats from Land's End whereas the conservative central banker may have little intention of going much beyond Keswick.

Worse was to come for the economist-engineers. In a series of hugely influential papers, Bob Lucas and people like Lionel Rapping and Tom Sargent, had considered the implications of rational expectations for policymaking. As already explained in this chapter, it was first necessary to try and locate the decision rules which underpinned the Phillips curve. Lucas suggested a rather attractive parable of workers, whose supply curves were a function of the relative rather than the absolute price of their production, and who simply could not tell whether any increase in the price of their product was an increase in all prices or simply an increase in their own product alone. With no central agency to tell them which was which, it was entirely likely that this confusion about absolute versus relative price changes would induce unwarranted increases in production; that is, agents might increase production in the production of a good, thinking that the higher price was signalling an incentive for more output. But eventually they would discover that they had misperceptions over the relative price and production would fall to the previous level.

This kind of thinking captured both the Humean observation that the overall price level, or inflation, did not matter in the long run as people would learn about the true source of the shock, but also that it might matter in the short run as people may make mistakes about value in the presence of price jumps.[10] In fact, the implication was that any short-term impact of any increases in inflation mattered for output only to the extent they were thought to be relative rather than absolute price changes. To the extent that large-scale monetary policy operations were always concerned with changes in the absolute price level, the increasing use of these would actually bias agents away from increasing production in the face of inflation shocks as agents began to assume that any change in price was an absolute rather than relative price change. These rational agents were going to be difficult to fool with systematic monetary policy. So the Phillips curve was not a trade-off between capacity and aggregate price pressure but actually the accidental result of inferences agents drew about the origin of any observed price shocks.

The next insight was even more astounding. Following Tinbergen-Theil, it had been the practice to estimate the structural relationships within and the economy and use these structural relationships to derive the optimal policy rule. A considerable effort had been placed in working out how to estimate key economic relationships from a system of equations and identify parameters in a manner that would allow some calculus of policy alternatives. But it turned out that the econometric evaluation of policy was fundamentally flawed. This is because once we tried to exploit the parameters of a previously estimated econometric relationship and change the policy rule in some manner, agents would tend to factor this new rule into their calculations and the previously estimated relationship would no longer hold.

---

[10] David Hume (1777) put it very well: 'that it is of no manner of consequence, with regard to the domestic happiness of a state, whether money be in a greater or less quantity'.

Could it be that the profession's contortions with different forms of the Phillips curve were not simply an attempt to locate the truth about the trade-off between capacity and inflation but were themselves a result of the way the economy changed as a result of changes in policy setting? And even worse, that systematic policy might be pretty much ineffective and that the costs of output volatility were not that great anyway; and all policy should do is to explain its plans to sceptical households and firms to the extent that these plans and objectives were incorporated in the plans of those people as a form of rule? Before I tell where we went to next, let me first tell you what went wrong as a result of all this newfangled 'fine tuning'.

4   A Science of Monetary Policy

*In which we arrive at a monetary policy parable or construct that seemed
to offer the answers. Almost corresponding intellectually to the idea that
governance in human history was driven toward Parliamentary
democracy, monetary policy was to be guided toward a framework of
controlling and managing the economy using rules.*

'Of what a strange nature is knowledge!
      It clings to the mind, when it has once seized on it, like a lichen on
the rock.'

Mary Shelley, *Frankenstein*, 1818

4.1   THE END OF MONETARY HISTORY?

Let me start at the end of this story. The end of monetary history was
supposed to be an independent central bank pursuing implicitly or explicitly an inflation target under the guise of operational independence. Other
aspects of financial policy and even fiscal policy could be partitioned off
into a box that said: Do Not Open. The central bank could pursue its target
in a rule-based manner and get agents to bind their behaviour with the
central bank's objectives. This alloy of jointly determined beliefs and
targets would tend to ensure stability in the face of shocks. It became not
so much a matter of getting people to do what you want but getting people
to do your job for you: if people always expected stability following any
sequence of shocks, they would not need so much proof from recessions
and painful interest rate hikes that central bankers really meant business.
Belief, even in a cynical age, can still be a powerful weapon.

However, the financial crisis had thrown that into sharp relief;
the question of whether monetary policy can be separated from other
aspects of financial and fiscal policy loomed large and has returned
with even more venom in the light of the COVID-19 crisis. It has
become increasingly difficult to argue with the proposition that financial regulation, fiscal policy and even the objectives of overseas policymakers, can all constrain the monetary policy makers' room for

manoeuvre. Indeed, in his June 2010 Mansion House speech, the then Governor of the Bank of England welcomed wholeheartedly the Chancellor's plan to recombine monetary and financial policy: 'the Bank (will) take on (responsibilities) in respect of micro prudential regulation and macro prudential control of the balance sheets of the financial system as a whole. I welcome those new responsibilities. Monetary stability and financial stability are two sides of the same coin. During the crisis the former was threatened by the failure to secure the latter'. Indeed, in the period immediately prior to the financial crisis a form of separation principle was in place, whereby monetary policy concentrated on one measure of macroeconomic disequilibria, inflation, that is, the rate at which consumer prices increase. This left financial or credit policy as a dull backwater, as it was perceived as essentially an aspect of microeconomic regulation.[1]

From an imaginary vantage point of the first few years of the twenty-first century, the collapse of the separation principle would seem rather more than surprising. The new monetary policy consensus that emerged seemed to have solved for all time, or timelessly, the many technical problems of monetary policy management. A representative view from this era, though written with circumspection, is that by Ben Bernanke (2004), who argued that:

> few disagree that monetary policy has played a large part in
> stabilizing inflation, and so the fact that output volatility has
> declined in parallel with inflation volatility, both in the United
> States and abroad, suggests that monetary policy may have helped
> moderate the variability of output as well ... my view is that
> improvements in monetary policy, though certainly not the only
> factor, have probably been an important source of the Great
> Moderation.

---

[1] Microeconomic (or Harberger) triangles of social losses will allow the calculation of welfare losses for financial matters and Okun Gaps (the deviation of output from potential) for monetary policy. It was usually felt that the latter will outweigh the former.

He suggests several reasons: (i) low and stable inflation outcomes promoting a more stable economic structure; (ii) better monetary policy may have reduced the size and distribution from which
measured shocks are drawn; and (iii) stable inflation expectations stop
becoming an exogenous driver of macroeconomic instability. But the
most important was arguably understanding simply the limitations of
monetary policy; that is, bound by severe information constraints
about the correct model of the economy and the state of nature,
monetary policy concentrated on simply gauging the correct current
level and prospective path of short-term interest rates in order to
stabilise aggregate demand over the medium term. A general accept-
ance that a simple rule was likely to dominate a full-blown optimal
control solution, which was, in any case, always predicated on a
particular model and not time consistent and subject to discretion,
or what used to be called 'fine-tuning'.[2]

From an older perspective, the *Art of Central Banking* predated
the *Science of Monetary Policy* and tended to define central banking
not so much in terms of a narrow price stability, but in terms of
objectives that might now be termed financial policy and involved
policies to safeguard the ongoing health of the financial system.[3] This
art developed as a response to both the multiplicity of roles 'grabbed'
by a maturing central bank and fundamentally in response to crises.
As already explained in this book, Walter Bagehot, author of *Lombard
Street* (1873), famously outlined the principles of central banking in a
crisis. The general understanding of these principles has been associated with the avoidance of banking panics in England since Overend
and Gurney (1866). Indeed, after Bagehot, Richard Sayers (1957) made
it rather clear how to frame central bank policy:

> The essence of central banking is discretionary control of the
> monetary system. The purpose of central banking has been defined
> in various ways: to maintain stability of the price level, to keep the

---

[2] See Fischer (1990).   [3] Clarida et al. (1999).

economy on an even keel, and so on ... The choice of purpose – the object of monetary policy – is not irrelevant to the choice of method: a community might hope more reasonably in some cases than in others to attain its ends by making the monetary system work to rule. And working to rule is the antithesis of central banking. A central bank is necessary only when the community decides that a discretionary element is desirable. The central banker is the man who exercises his discretion, not the machine that works according to rule.

Indeed, discretionary short-term liquidity support, of varying kinds, was ultimately offered by all major central banks following the August 2007 freeze in the interbank markets, in the aftermath of the Brexit referendum result and the eruption of the COVID-19 crisis. Another issue emerged in 2008 that we have not quite solved: how to deal with the problem that it is quite hard to get nominal interest rates on bank deposits significantly below zero because our old friend money, which is the alternative to holding an interest-bearing bank account, always pays a nominal interest rate of zero? In each case, the response has been to increase the size of the central bank balance sheet. The basic idea here has borrowed from an older literature in which the size, composition and risk taken by the central bank onto its balance sheet is used to control financial conditions more generally. Because of imperfect substitutability across financial claims, a central bank that uses it balance sheet to alter the structure of private sector balance sheets and market segmentation can influence financial prices (James Tobin, 1969) and hence affects monetary and financial conditions, by which I mean the set of interest rates, financial prices and loan availability that is part of the transmission mechanism from the monetary to the real sectors. This leads to the question of the extent to which balance sheet operations, and commercial bank reserve policy, are indeed instruments independent of the short-term interest rate, but we shall leave this matter to the next chapter.

The financial crisis injected a considerable degree of variance into the economic belief system. In the eyes of many it would appear that an economic crisis necessarily implies a crisis in economics itself; so much so that many question not only the relevance of trying to use deeper microeconomic principles, or foundations, in order to understand economic behaviour in the aggregate but are even also ascribing a causal role from the over-reliance on economic models, or one type of economic model, as a contributory factor in the crisis itself. Bad ideas, even when well put, can damage economies. I will argue that although there had been too much reliance on one type of simple model, the methodology implied by that model has not been shown to be flawed.

In fact, the challenge faced by the economists really stem from two basic errors. The first error has been to over analyse the policy implication of a simple New Keynesian model in which the basic rigidity has only effectively involved some forms of price stickiness and very little else. The second has been to compound the problem by spending extensive resources trying to estimate forms of this model, and then to use them to underpin policy formulation rather than develop a more convincing structure in which informational and financial frictions trigger significantly different responses to economic shocks. These errors made it nearly impossible to develop fully a richer vein of models that yield the kind of policy prescriptions chosen, in a hurry and in the dark, in response to the global financial crisis. In this chapter I shall try to explain how we ended up with such an alarmingly simple, perhaps over simplistic, yet for such a long time a seemingly effective approach.

4.2   THE RECORD

The UK post-war macroeconomic record, although common knowledge, is worth a re-examination. Figure 4.1 shows the year-on-year growth in real GDP and in a broad-based measure of the prices, the GDP deflator. From the mid-1950s to the end of the Bretton Woods system of fixed but adjustable exchange rates, we can observe reasonable levels of GDP growth and passable attempts to maintain price ability. But let me point to two observations, every successive peak in

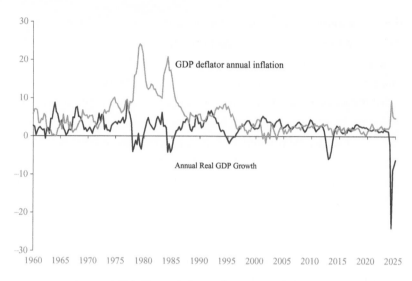

FIGURE 4.1 UK inflation and growth

inflation was higher and prior to 1971 the peaks in output growth were also lower. After the abandonment of fixed exchange rates, the downward shock to potential output growth in the early 1970s was treated as a demand deficient phenomenon and, without a firm nominal anchor for prices and wage settlement, expansionary policies generated high and persistent levels of inflation. The disinflation of the 1980s was associated with a further recession but again, with no credible nominal anchor, the subsequent boom of the late 1980s led to both higher inflation and the abandonment of a domestic nominal anchor by joining the ERM.[4] By doing so we announced that we did not have the domestic institutional capability; with hindsight that was quite a statement with the Bank of England approaching its tercentenary. The adoption of inflation targeting in 1992 heralded in a period of exceptional stability with low inflation and stable growth. Of course, the good times ended in 2007 with year-on-year growth at − 6 per cent in the first quarter of 2009. Since then we have been caught

---

[4] The ERM is shorthand for the European Exchange Rate Mechanism of the European Monetary System.

in a period of sustained low growth in what might be best described as latter-day doldrums. This has created little or no room for a normalisation in Bank Rate as shock after shock has pinned us back in the position we reached shortly after the financial crisis. A policy sump rather than an economic slump.

There has been much talk about how to measure aggregate welfare and in most macroeconomic models, the policymaker, taking a steer from society, is thought to care about inflation and output deviations from target or steady state, which we might translate crudely into an index adding up the two sets of standard deviations, which is a statistical measure of the dispersion in the respective time series. Obviously there are many objections to such a measure as we might be interested in distributional issues and in other measures of welfare, such as consumption growth or real household net disposable income. However, even when we use models with deep microeconomic foundations based on optimising over the households budget constraint, we tend to find that welfare does tend to be (inversely) proportional to some weighted average of inflation and output growth. So in Figure 4.2, I show a simple misery index, which does not add the level of inflation with that of unemployment but plots the rolling five-year simple sum of the standard deviations in inflation and output growth. Naturally, the weights, in this case 1 to 1, can be disputed, as can the choice of the Parliament–inspired five-year horizon – it is arbitrary – but the index is perhaps a convenient way of thinking about measuring the uncertainty about economic performance and a proxy for damage this causes to general economic welfare. Overall, prior to 2020, there seems to be something of a downward trend, suggesting that macroeconomic management by and large may be improving, but clearly there are significant events that upset the monetary and financial settlement and have triggered an interest in policymakers for redesigning the monetary policy framework.

Let us take another type of slice through this data by scattering the data in different sub-periods in Figure 4.3. In the top left panel I show the Bretton Woods period; in the top right panel the period

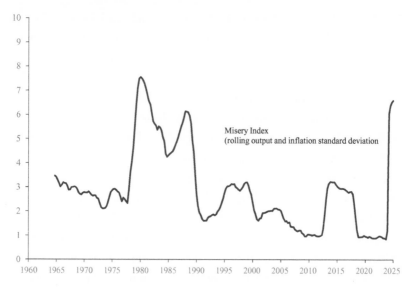

FIGURE 4.2 Measuring misery in the United Kingdom

which we might describe as the quest for a nominal anchor; the bottom left is the classical inflation targeting period over the long expansion; and in the bottom right the period trough which we are now living. A standard view is that inflation should not be related to growth other than temporarily so that over long-run periods we ought not to see any significant relationship. The Phillips curve, as we discussed in the previous chapter, is a short-run trade-off that will disappear over time as growth returns to its long-run level. What I think we can see when we move from the north-west to north-east quadrant is that the range of outcomes for both output and inflation become considerably wider and, in particular, the loss of a nominal anchor means that shocks are transmitted to nominal outcomes in a persistent manner.

In fact, it looks like the whole economy pivoted onto a higher level of inflation – stagflation – with a reduction in the medium-term rate of growth. Against these developments the subsequent compression of outcomes looks quite remarkable: for a fifteen-year period, practically a generation, inflation and output seemed boxed into

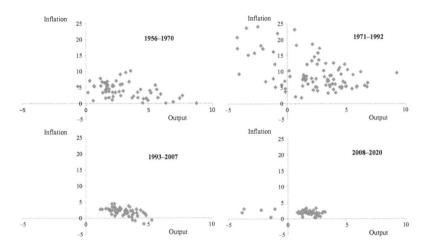

FIGURE 4.3 Inflation and growth outcomes

positive levels under 5 per cent. The negative income shocks associated with the financial crisis have been large, but the second remarkable observation to make is that nominal anchor has done its job. There has been no loss (yet) of monetary stability as there was in the 1970s and 1980s. Let us hope that we stay in the neighbourhood of these outcomes as we emerge from the COVID-19 cloud.

4.3   HUMEAN LUCAS

As we have already noted, the long run neutrality of money is a central plank of monetary policymaking (Lucas, 1995). As is well known, the insight dates back to at least David Hume, who made exactly the same point – albeit rather more elegantly than I just did – in the first sentence. Although it is quite a simple matter to find long-run non-neutralities in many standard models, it is generally found that long-run non-neutralities should not be exploited as there is not any clear enhancement in the welfare of the representative household as that depends on things like real wages and leisure time. Naturally though, perturbations in the money market will lead to temporary changes in the market-clearing level of (overnight or short-term) policy rates and, because of various forms of informational uncertainty or structural rigidity, will lead to temporary deviations in the expected real rate from its natural level and thus act on aggregate demand. And so the key question is the extent to which shocks emanating from the money market can be stabilised by an interest rate rule or indeed whether an additional tool may required. So in the long run, the value of money was determined by its relative scarcity and would do nothing to change real endowments, preferences and relative prices of goods and services. Indeed, Hume went even further to suggest a way for monetary policy to be thought about:

> From the whole of this reasoning we may conclude, that it is of no manner of consequence, with regard to the domestic happiness of a state, whether money be in a greater or less quantity. The good policy of the magistrate consists only in keeping it, if possible, still increasing; because, by that means, he keeps alive a spirit of industry in the nation, and increases the stock of labour, in which consists all real power and riches.

He had observed that because of money's long-run neutrality it does not affect welfare, but by ensuring that it is circulated in a manner to keep trade and industry going it can help, and perhaps I over interpret, smooth the business cycle.

The observation about neutrality is important because if we cannot permanently effect output with a monetary policy, what can we do? The new classical reply is along the lines of *primum non nocere*, or first, do no harm. Perhaps the person at the vanguard of this response was Bob Lucas, so let us examine his contributions. There are two aspects of Lucas' thought I want to place before you. The first is simply about the costs of business cycle fluctuations and what value we might wish to place on stabilisation policy. Using a simple calculation and the assumption that we can examine the average household as a representative one, we can examine the cost of the expected standard deviation in terms of the average level of consumption of this average household. We can ask ourselves how much income would the representative household be willing to give up in order to eliminate the standard deviation of their year-to-year changes in consumption of goods and services. It turns out that it is not very much, typically, a small fraction of 1 per cent of the level of overall consumption per head, because the standard deviation of average consumption growth does not turn out to be particularly high and households, although risk averse, are not especially paranoid (yet).

Secondly, in a justly famous paper, Lucas (1976) criticised the econometric evaluation of policy of the type outlined by Tinbergen-Theil. The argument takes the following form.

- The policymaker may estimate certain behavioural parameters, for example, how much inflation may flow from a given increase in output;
- If they have some notion of establishing price stability at some implicit level of inflation they may decide to respond to any observed increases in output using their estimates of the responsiveness of inflation to output and of the impact their policy instrument has in output;
- The problem Lucas highlighted was a circularity: the calculation of the optimal response of the policymaker depending on estimates that themselves contained previous responses of policymakers;
- If the policymaker now changed her behaviour, the estimates based on historic behaviour not only would be wrong, but the response of the economy may not have the expected effect.

A variant of the idea emerged from Charles Goodhart, who argued that once a targeted quantity becomes the objective of policy, it ceases to carry quite the same special value as it had before. The point carries through to targets in the provision of many public goods from schools' performance to NHS waiting lists or tests for COVID-19. Let me illustrate with a contemporary example depicted in Figure 4.4. A goalkeeper wanting to decide a policy about whether to dive to his right or left against a particular forward might think statistics produced by an econometrician may help. First he might pay someone to examine the success rate of a particular forward and work out if they tended to score when they shot to the goalkeeper's left or right. The goalkeeper can then act armed with the knowledge that the forward scores when he shoots to the goalkeeper's left. Naturally, the next

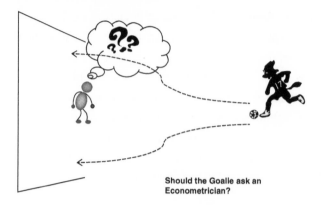

Should the Goalie ask an
Econometrician?

FIGURE 4.4 The Lucas critique and the penalty shoot-out

time he faces a penalty from this forward, he dives to his left and saves it. And that is the Tinbergen-Theil argument: the goalkeeper has a preference to save the goal; he knows the structure of the forward's shooting plans and can implement a policy to meet the preference, that is, dive to his left. However, Lucas says something quite different. If the forward also has access to the published information about his success rate and works out that the goalkeeper he is about to take a penalty against will dive to his left, the forward has an incentive to change his behaviour. He will re-optimise, shoot to the goalkeeper's right, score and knock England out of the World Cup.[5] The optimality of the 'estimated' penalty saving reaction function disappears in a Lucasian puff of logic.

One way to square this circle is to find a response, or reaction function, that does not depend on estimated parameters that are also a function of previous rules. But locating a story in which the behaviour of the economy in terms of price- and wage-setting behaviour or the determination of financial contracts can be thought to be independent of the monetary rule, seems to me to be quite hard. Another option may be to avoid any form of feedback rule and just adopt non-discretionary or even random response. Our goalkeeper will do better

___

[5] Or loose the Euro 2020 final held in 2021!

by randomising his responses so that the penalty taker just does not know where he will dive. So we are left with a number of important principles. First, remember that changing the growth rate of money will not affect growth and productivity in any significant manner for the better; secondly, perhaps because of private and public insurance, households do not seem to face extremely high levels of aggregate risk on average; and thirdly, beware of fine-tuning responses in an economy that will learn about what you do and may even nullify the impact.

4.4   RATIONAL EXPECTATIONS AND POLICYMAKING

If elements of the Lucas critique sound a bit like portrayals of efficient markets, in which all information gets publicly traded and this makes it quite hard for agents to make excess profits or for people like central bankers to influence behaviour, actually they are. The so-called rational expectations revolution was taking a firm grip on economics and monetary policy making by this time. Perhaps the most obvious or clear point would be the one raised by Sargent and Wallace (1975), called the policy ineffectiveness proposition, which states that policy that relies on any feedback from observed data cannot affect the plans of people who have already used that observed data to work out their preferred course of action. If policymakers, households and firms both have access to the same information set and have freedom to act optimally with that information, how can policymakers 'fool' households or firms into working more or less hours or producing more or fewer goods?

Let us treat the information set for policymakers and the private sector as public and known to both. If the policymaker decides to respond systematically to lower output by increasing the rate of issuance of money in order to offset some of the fall in output, we might reasonably expect agents to forecast this increase in money supply growth and consequently a higher inflation rate and start to ask for higher money wages to compensate themselves for the fall in the value of money. Should prices and wages jump in proportion to the change in the money supply, nothing real will change and the policy gambit would have been finessed.

Without jumping to the final punchline, one response by the policymaker would be to enter a world of mystique, opacity and near secrecy; a world of central bank magic conjuring up stability on demand like so many doves. Or where decisions emerge as white smoke rising above the London skyline. They may decide that their own analysis and models are part of the private sector's information set and that it might be best not to explain very clearly how data gets turned into policy responses. This magic circle mystique may leave the private sector without much ability to forecast when policy might respond to events and so we have a regime of policy surprises. One possible response of the policy world to the natural implications of a full information place might be to try and make that world a little less of a full information world and thus hold on to some residual power to effect policy by stealth. I do not think that policy by mystique is a credible way ahead because it relies on the view that agents cannot learn; that central banks do not have a duty to explain the principles behind their actions in advance; and that the kind of equilibrium we end up in when the private sector and the central bank play a game of bluff and counter-bluff is preferable to one in which they can through persuasion and understanding agree on common objectives and move jointly towards them. The latter path is the one consistent with democratic accountability.

The next set of principles flowed from the work of Kydland and Prescott (1977) and Barro and Gordon (1983). The former pair launched a full-frontal salvo against the rationale behind any attempt to apply elements of control theory to rational, forward-looking agents. They argued that unlike the natural world, in which the game is between agents who do not learn or forecast your responses, the game of economic policy will force policymakers to abandon seemingly optimal plans. The argument is rather subtle but hugely important nevertheless. Imagine a policymaker, who wishes to maximise output growth and decides to allow capital to migrate into their

Table 4.1. *The pay-offs from the private sector central bank game*

		Central Bank	
		Low	High
Private Sector	Low	Bliss Point	High Output
	High	Low Output	Inflation Bias

The good equilibrium (Bliss Point) is unstable because the Central Bank has an incentive to deviate and the private sector can see that.

country in order to increase productive capacity; this is basically what many emerging economies did in the aftermath of the global financial crisis. The policymaker may announce a plan to set capital taxes to zero and this policy will produce the required large flow of capital. But as the stock of capital increases, the policymaker may have revenues to raise for roads to be built, for example, and may be faced with an increasingly tempting incentive to change policy and tax the now burgeoning, and sticky, capital stock. In fact when the returns from changing policy outweigh those from maintaining the status quo, for example, in the run up to an election, the policymaker will snap and raise capital taxes. Now here is the rub. The capital investors should be able to work out now that some future trigger point will force a change in the ability of a government to stick to its plans and so will work on the basis that taxes will be raised, despite whatever the government says. As a result, and without a form of institutions that can provide a credible commitment technology to maintain low or zero taxes, not that much capital will not flow into the country in the first place. The government can say whatever it wants to mobile capitalists but it will not succeed without an ability to inspire credibility in its announced plans. A country with a large debt burden and significant taxes to raise may find foreign direct investment incredibly scarce.

Barro and Gordon applied this idea to a simple monetary policy game in which the policymaker has an objective for low inflation and stable output growth, but rather like Oliver Twist, wants some more output growth, if at all possible. We illustrate the possibilities in Table 4.1. If the policymaker announces a target for low and stable inflation, as a wage bargainer I have two alternative responses. Do I believe – giving him or her credibility – the policymaker and hold my wage growth in line with the target? If I do so and there is a stable pact then we are at our old Bliss Point. Or do I choose to cast doubt on the policymaker because I think they may gain from reneging on their plan or target. My rational response will not only look at the benefits to me from my two choices but also the benefits to the policymaker from playing within the rules or acting with discretion.

The policymaker can also do the same exercise. They can hold policy firm to meet the target or re-optimise on the private sector's credibility and renege. The box shows the four possible outcomes. There are two equilibria in which both sides play the same cards. Under credibility, the private sector believes in the target and acts accordingly with nominal wages set in line with the full employment level for real wages. In this case the central bank hits the target as well and the world is a happy, smiling place. Now consider the incentives: if the private sector bargains for higher nominal wages they will also lead to higher real wages for those who have jobs – although his or her wages will lead to lower levels of output as fewer workers are hired.

Alternatively, the central bank could engineer more output by having a surprise inflation that would lower real wages and increase the quantity of employment and hence output. If the private sector bargains for high wage rates, then the only way we have full employment is for the central bank to meet those requirements and raise inflation, and if the central bank is observed to have an incentive to induce a surprise inflation, then that is precisely what the private sector will expect. The low inflation equilibrium is thus very unstable and will tend to the high inflation state, because both parties have an incentive to plan around the high inflation state and create, what was termed, an inflation bias. Again in the absence of a credible commitment technology, the economy cannot achieve a lasting degree of price stability. This inflation bias will therefore persist without fundamental institutional reform.

The rational expectations revolution had led to a fundamental change in the requirements for a policymaker. We needed to write down an economic model in which agents could learn or forecast the policymaker's responses. We also had an obligation to spell out the policymaker's objectives and explain the reaction function in terms of its arguments and its instruments, and ideally society demanded a target, or fixed point, about which all agents would co-ordinate permanently and this target would be stable simply because there were no obvious long-run benefits for either side from doing otherwise.

4.5   THE SEARCH FOR A NOMINAL ANCHOR

The story of the United Kingdom's search for a nominal anchor is probably worthy of a book in its own right, as it was a rather tortuous process of parable and nightmare. The end of the Bretton Woods regime of fixed but adjustable exchange rates versus the US dollar left domestic monetary policymakers with a choice over which domestic nominal targets to adopt. The starting point was some form of caps on both wage and price increases. Such aggregate targets tend to prevent relative price adjustment and in the wake of a dislocated monetary anchor, the falls in real wages meant that there had been a large incentive for nominal wage contracts to be repriced upwards. A continuing deterioration of the fiscal position made the domestic achievement of macroeconomic stability almost impossible and the IMF were called in to provide some form of credible commitment technology. About this time, the first set of money targets were adopted and under the medium-term financial strategy of the 1980s, involved an evolving sequence of choices and debates about the correct quantity of money to target.

It turned out that targeting the money stock in some narrow or ever-wider form was not a particularly good idea in the presence of ferocious financial innovation and reform, which regularly changed the relationship between money, its close substitutes and total transactions. Furthermore, money targeting was always going to be a pretty good example of the Lucas critique, or what we also termed Goodhart's Law: as soon as you try to target an intermediate quantity or price in order to achieve a particularly final objective, the link between intermediate and final objective will be irrevocably broken. The observation tends to carry over to all kinds of targets in the public sector for schools, hospitals and even assessments of university lecturers. The evolving experiment with a domestic nominal anchor ended with the start of the late 1980s boom, which was exacerbated by the shadowing of the Deutsche Mark and brought to an abrupt end by the firm, but not sustainable, adoption of another exchange rate peg within the European Exchange Rate Mechanism (ERM) in October 1990. The credible commitment technology could not, it seems, be found at home, so it was necessary to rent (shadow) and then buy (join the ERM) one from abroad. The very best was bought from the Bundesbank. As Circe warned Ulysses:

> You will come to the Sirens who enchant all who come near them.
> If any one unwarily draws in too close and hears the singing of the
> Sirens, his wife and children will never welcome him home
> again . . . therefore pass these Sirens by . . . and bind you[rself] as you
> stand upright on a cross piece half way up the mast.
>
> (Homer, trans. Butler, 1952, p. 250)

In fact, even the Bundesbank could not be relied upon to meet its intermediate target, as the impact of reunification threw the monetary numbers off track, as we show in Figure 4.5, taken from Richard Clarida and Mark Gertler (1997). Here is the nice thing about credibility, it should be able to withstand temporary shocks or aberrations and may lead to a faster bind.

The ERM exit in September 1992 meant that a domestic nominal anchor had to be found and we adopted, almost overnight – well over three weeks – flexible inflation targets in October 1992. Under Inflation Targeting I, policy rates were set by the chancellor. After the adoption of operational independence in May 1997, Inflation

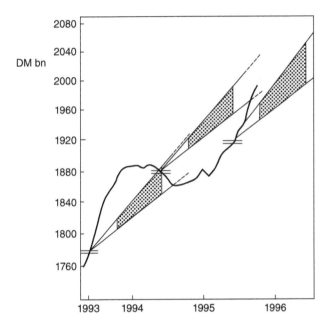

FIGURE 4.5 German M3 growth relative to target

Targeting II, policy rates were set by the MPC to a target set by the Executive. We have already examined the outcomes under this regime and it would seem fair to think that we have found a stable form of anchor. The reforms after the financial crisis to ensure that monetary, fiscal and financial policy co-ordinate may yet lead to a more complex regime, but for the moment, monetary policy is still judged by the likely attainment of low and stable inflation both currently and in expectation. There will be calls to change the remit if it is judged that the consequences are inherently political, redis-tributive or acting as a substitute for fiscal policies, but central banks can only affect nominal magnitudes in the long run, not relative resource allocations.

4.6 'BY JOVE, I THINK SHE'S GOT IT'

The macroeconomic relationships that were not derived from first principles and mostly posited from observation, introspection or estimation were shunned by the new generation of macroeconomists who demanded models with microeconomic foundations. This meant that models had to be derived from the basic principles of the maximisation of household utility subject per period income and borrowing constraints; firm level behaviour that also sought to maximise profits subject to the costs of production and the posted prices of output; and, where specified, monetary and fiscal policies were sequences of interest rate choices and budget deficits, and surpluses that did not violate the government's own budget constraint in the long run. As I am concerned with telling a story about monetary policy, we shall concentrate on the application of this new way of thinking about macroeconomics to the monetary policy problem.

The point of departure for a simple macroeconomic model suitable for monetary policy analysis became the New Keynesian (NK) framework (see Bennett McCallum, 2001), which is essentially an aggregate model with dominant supply side dynamics but where sticky prices mean that output may deviate temporarily from its long-run level, by which time prices are fully flexible. This deviation, of current output from its long-run equilibrium, is the output gap which has throughout our examination of policy been the key indicator of inflation and the motivation for monetary policy action. The possibility of temporary deviations in output from its flex-price level creates a role for the monetary policymaker. In brief, the basic NK story is that the capacity of output is set by a production function based on usual arguments in land and capital with its accumulation of efficiency shocks (see, for example, the so-called Solow residuals, 1987) and short-run output is determined by a monopolistically competitive supply side faced with an ability only to change their prices at a particular moment in what is called time-dependent price setting, or following a paper by Guillermo Calvo, Calvo price setting.

The NK structure means that the full capacity level of output in this economy lies at a point below the perfectly competitive frontier, which in principle provides an incentive to push the economy above its capacity level. Secondly, with prices adjusting only gradually to an optimal, or target, mark-up over evolving marginal costs, short-run output can deviate from this full capacity level. Following any shocks, prices can only be reset in each period by the fraction of firms who are sent an exogenous (Calvo) signal to reprice – with some fraction in each time period. So all other firms are faced with having to accept a suboptimal price for their output for at least one period and the overall price level, which is a combination of all firm prices, is also suboptimal, which means that there are both distributional and direct output consequences from sticky prices. To help us understand the consequences let's think through the following thought experiment. For a given change in costs, all firms would wish to change prices and maintain an optimal mark-up, but if only some fraction can, those that cannot will lose out and welfare losses will reflect the size of the gap and the speed at which the population of firms can adjust. If the central bank can engineer price stability in the face of shocks, these losses will be limited.

Inflation is driven by both the difference between capacity and the short-run aggregate level of production chosen by all firms and expected inflation. And so inflation, at least in its temporary deviations from target, is not a monetary phenomenon in this model but really an output gap or mark-up phenomenon, which is itself controlled by interest rate choices. Nevertheless, to this basic model we can also consider appending a simple model of money demand (for which supply by the monetary policymaker is implicitly perfectly elastic), where we assume that households need to hold money balances to meet a given level of planned nominal expenditures. The role of the policymaker is to set interest rates so that output stabilises at the capacity level, that is, the so-called output gap is closed, at which point inflation is also stabilised.

This model deals with a number of issues highlighted in this book so far. Firms and household are rational in the sense that they set prices and plans rationally and in a forward-looking manner. But it is the combination of monopolistic competition, which gives firms some pricing power over their mark-ups, and sticky prices that means

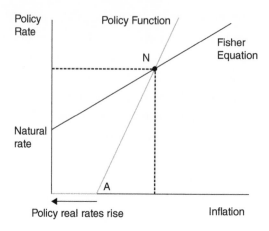

FIGURE 4.6 Setting New Keynesian policy

that output can deviate from its long-run level in a manner resembling a business cycle. In this model, it is possible to write the output gap as a function of the expected output gap plus the real interest rate and inflation as a function of expected inflation and the output gap. In fact we can then write inflation as a function of the expected stream of output gaps or indeed the stream of policy rates themselves. The forward-looking agents can use the path of expected interest rates to guide their views about future inflation back to target. It is as beautiful as a perfect circle drawn by Leonardo da Vinci.

Let us to try to show how this process might work graphically in Figure 4.6. The New Keynesian Policymaker had a simple, basic picture at the back of their minds when thinking about monetary policy. There is an inflation target where the thick dotted line meets the horizontal axis. When we add back in the natural rate of interest or the neutral real interest rate, we then arrive at the steady state policy rate, where the thick dotted line meets the x-axis. Point N gives the normal equilibrium here with an inflation target and a long run natural interest rate. The natural rate of interest is that which clears the market for savings and investment. The line labelled 'Fisher Equation' simply adds a nominal return onto the natural rate of interest defined at the expected inflation rate, which for the purposes of simplicity we set equal to the actual inflation rate plus some random error. All points along the line labelled Fisher Equation imply the same real or neutral real interest rate and so do not impact on aggregate demand, which is a negative function of deviations in the policy rate from this real rate. Off chart, perturbations from aggregate demand relative to supply lead to inflation. The policy function therefore is steeper than the Fisher Equation line and it brings aggregate demand down when there is upwards inflationary pressure and vice versa.

In this rather mechanistic setting we can understand the impact of changes to, for example, the natural rate, which implies a shift up in the intercept of the Fisher Equation and also a shift upwards to the left for the policy function at a given inflation rate. We can also quickly understand why a mistaken belief that the natural rate, which cannot be observed, is increasing, can lead rather quickly to problems, as policy rates may be left too low for too long, excessively stimulating demand. Whilst the possibility of uncertainty about the natural rate was clear, we were unable to say anything very much about how to identify changes in it or even think in a constructive manner about the correct set of market interest rates that might allow us to understand the neutral rate.

Still, setting aside the two great real-time unmeasurables, the output gap and the neutral rate of interest, it seemed inflation and aggregated demand relative to supply, could be stabilized if policy was sufficiently forward-looking. At point A, though, things change. Here nominal rates cannot fall with inflation, and ever-larger negative output gaps, driving down inflation, will thereby increase real rates and so in principle set up a destabilising feedback loop – unless something else can be found to ease monetary and financial conditions. These instruments turned out first to be a large depreciation in the exchange rate and, with more novelty, quantitative easing, which led to a large, persistent but temporary expansion of the central bank balance, but facilitated considerable influence on long term interest rates.

4.7   FROM ART TO SCIENCE AND BACK AGAIN

So the simple linearised New Keynesian model both succeeded and failed. It succeeded because the policy reaction function simply has to react by more than any given change in inflation so that the real interest rate acts to bear down on any output gap and drive inflation back to its target. It also provided a set of macroeconomic principles grounded in microeconomic theory as the model was derived from first principles and the target seemed likely to minimise the social losses from business cycle fluctuations. Belief in the target and ability of the central bank to hit it seemed to have ended any further search for monetary rules.

But the model also fails along a number of dimensions because this linear model is subject to a number of well-known words, control problems, which were exposed in the financial crisis: (i) changes in the natural rate (the intercept), which cannot be easily measured, will lead to monetary impulses from nominal rates that imply an incorrect real rate of interest; (ii) measuring the output gap and then forecasting the change in the inflation rate that is implied is very difficult in real-time; (iii) with no set of asset prices in the model, we are left hoping that use of a single policy rate leads to clearing in credit markets that does not leave the economy in a fragile state; and (iv) finally if rates were to fall to zero and deflationary pressures continued to escalate, real rates would rise and the economy would be in serious danger of not being able to be stabilised.

Actually, the failures exposed by the financial crisis were simply that financial risks had built up in a manner that threatened the integrity of the whole system, what we might call a very large shock. Throughout the crisis, this form of model helped us think about the appropriate response. One set of responses involved under-standing that forward-looking agents need to be told what the end point is. And that one possible exit from the crisis might be a boom, so we might be able to escape if the authorities committed to a boom by promising to hold interest rates below the neutral level for an extended period – in general such a commitment had not been forth-coming. Cautious central bankers have relied on rough estimates of the likely responses of the monetary transmission mechanism to asset purchases to try and generate impacts analogous to those that might have happened if policy rates could have gone substantially negative. Without a robust model of cause and effect for asset prices and finan-cial factors in the transmission mechanism at hand, this is where to some degree we can question the science and realise that balancing so many alternate choices may require the canvas of art. The lag here was that theory seemed far behind the needs of a crisis and needed to catch up and fast.

5 Where the Great Experiment Went Wrong

In which we examine whether we could really expect to end boom and bust with central bank independence. How asset prices, in particular those of houses, became the focus of a debate that missed the growing fragility in the banking and financial system. Would a closer examination of monetary behaviour have helped or was a stable inflation rate considered to be the sole limit of central bank ambition?

Nothing is built on stone; All is built on sand, but we must build as if the sand were stone.

Jorge Luis Borges, *Poemas*, 1923-58

5.1 TO END BOOM AND BUST

One of the interesting canards, perhaps as a result of the inflationary episodes of the 1970s and 1980s, was that price stability rapidly developed into a sufficient statistic to judge whether a macroeconomic equilibrium had been achieved. In both the public arena and the policy sphere, the continuing attainment of low and stable rates of inflation seemed to suggest that monetary policy had not only functioned well but perhaps had discovered the key 'to end boom and bust'. Indeed, the then chancellor, Gordon Brown, summed up the view well, which was very much the overall consensus at the time, in a speech to the British Chamber of Commerce in 2000:

> it was to avoid the historic British problem – the violence of the
> repeated boom and bust cycles of the past – that we established the
> new monetary framework based on consistent rules – the
> symmetrical inflation target; settled well-understood procedures –
> bank independence; and openness and transparency. And side by
> side with it and as important, a new fiscal discipline with, again,
> clear and consistent rules – the golden rule for public spending; well

understood procedures – our fiscal responsibility legislation; and a new openness and transparency.

In most of the models or parables we have rehearsed, persistent deviation in inflation from target can only occur if current or expected aggregate demand is persistently greater than potential output. Given that policy tends to stabilise demand through a sequence of predictable responses to any excessive demands, such a persistent deviation can only result from a faulty or mistaken interpretation by policymakers of the state of demand relative to supply. Although it is actually very hard to disentangle demand from supply shocks in real time – so much so that a large fraction of policymaker's time is spent trying to do just that – we might reasonably expect such judgements to not be persistently wrong – as learning about the current state and the most recent states of nature may be thought to become easier as time passes, and todays become yesterdays. So if volatile inflation is just a policy error, if it is stable, are there no policy errors?

Naturally, examining far ahead inflation expectations can be one way to judge whether households and firms believe that policy will react sufficiently to any dislocations in demand and supply. Over the long expansion of 1992–2007, surveys of firm and household inflation expectations were indeed boringly stable, as were expectations derived from the prices of nominal and inflation-proofed government bonds as shown in Figure 5.1. However, such an observation does not necessarily make the job of the policymaker so easy that they can go off to the beach. First the inflation expectations themselves may contain an expectation that policy will respond to any current and future shocks so that the resulting inflation rate five or ten years ahead remains on track. The stable level of inflation expectations does not say that nothing needs to be done, but there is some trust that the right things will continue to be done. Secondly, in a forward-looking model, stable inflation expectations simply imply that the positive and negative output gaps cancel each other out and allow us to say very little about the implied path of the output gap period by period.

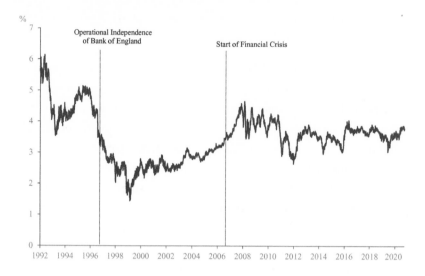

FIGURE 5.1 Long horizon inflation expectations over the long expansion

One way to think about the stable inflation expectations, which may seem rather unlikely, is that the noughties boom was balanced by a forecast of the subsequent recession, and in the middle of all this expected volatility in output, inflation remained stable.

Before we start to think that there had been any kind of benign neglect of financial imbalances in the monetary policy debates prior to the crash, let me explain the tenor of the debate. There had been in fact a huge discussion amongst monetary economists about whether inflation targeting was sufficient or whether some innovation implying flexible inflation targeting was required or, indeed, whether the arguments in the policymaker's reaction function should be augmented to include factors such as asset prices or financial balances, real income or its distribution, and more recently whether there should be a green argument in its reaction function. The classic and simple view of inflation targeting is the straw man I developed in the previous chapter, where the central bank just seeks to bring inflation back to target over the forecast horizon with little or no regard for any output variance. The flexible inflation targeter will aim to stabilise both inflation and the real economy and will be willing to accept some trade-off between inflation and output variance. Some economists went further and argued that financial and monetary variables are not only information variables about the state of the economy but can be used as target variables in their own right. At some point these different approaches seem to converge and that is because the basic models did not articulate how a financial sector might amplify rather than attenuate shocks, and how risk-taking may lead to a highly unstable system. We did not really have any kind of model that articulated the view of Andrew Crockett, then managing director of the Basle-based Bank for International Settlements (BIS), that: the received wisdom is that risk increases in recessions and falls in booms. In contrast, it may be more helpful to think of risk as increasing during upswings, as financial imbalances build up, and materialising in recessions.

That something went wrong is now clear. The long-run performance of the economy after 2007 perhaps could not have been predicted given the performance in the fifteen-year-long expansion from 1992. Yet the whole thrust of the various debates we have examined on stabilisation policy have been formulated with the objective of creating stability. The ride since 2007 could be described as anything but stable. We are therefore left wondering whether the previous period of stability was really a chimera? As Dennis Robertson wrote in 1922: 'Money is not such a vital subject as often supposed ... A monetary system is like some internal organ; it should not be allowed to take up very much of our thoughts when it goes right, but needs a great deal of attention when it goes wrong.'

5.2 INDEPENDENCE DAY FOR THE OLD LADY

In the previous chapter we looked at the remarkable period of real income and inflation performance that provided the context, and to some extent, the diagnostic, on the Long Expansion that ended so abruptly and the financial crisis, which led to the doldrumic growth episode prior to the COVID-19 crisis. The inflation targeting regime established in October 1992 started first with a wide band of 1–4 per cent for RPI (Retail Price Index) inflation excluding mortgage interest payments, the wide band being somewhat reminiscent of the bands for oft-changed money targets. However, there was an additional constraint that involved reaching a level below 2.5 per cent by the end of that Parliament. By 1995 this target was modified to 2.5 per cent; when the target was moved from RPI to CPI (Consumer Price Index) in December 2003, the target was once again changed to 2 per cent. Under both targets, from 1997 onwards there was a 1 per cent band of error allowed before the Governor's pencil would have to be sharpened for letter writing to explain why inflation had fallen outside its band and when it would return.

The move from RPI to CPI was quite sensible but the collective memory can be quite durable. The RPI has a long history. It was first calculated as an interim measure in June 1947; made official in 1956; and has, for successive generations, become the focal point for trying to understand the change in the overall price of a representative basket of goods bought by households. This understanding of general price inflation through the veil of RPI continues to permeate the formation of contracts both in the public and private sectors. Yet this index is widely thought to be flawed as a measure of general inflation, as at times it can greatly overestimate and at other times underestimate changes in prices faced by households.

Despite its major shortfall as a measure of inflation, the one crumb of comfort is that in the very long run various price indices of the costs of living tend to have the same long-run properties and, hence, move together. So for very long-run analysis of broad trend the RPI series may not be so problematic, but in the short run, which can mean a sequence of several years, series such as the RPI and CPI (published from 1996 and 'modelled' on an experimental basis back to 1949) may drift apart and this may have important consequences for households whose annual increments to costs and income may be linked to quite different measures of price inflation.

The most serious problem with the RPI concerns the predominant use of the simple average across all price changes rather than the use of the geometric mean, which is the dominant method for calculating the CPI, and is more appropriate for data where there is volatility and serial correlation in individual price series. In general, the absolute inflation rate under the geometric mean is smaller than under the arithmetic mean. The second problem is that the RPI treatment of housing costs uses mortgage interest rate payments and house prices rather than a measure of owner occupiers' housing costs, which are now calculated and included in an additional measure of consumer price inflation, CPIH. Note that these two measures of housing costs rarely agree, but the latter estimate of owner occupiers' housing costs is preferable. We shall return to the question of housing costs shortly.

The critical development was not just the adoption of a target but the executive offering operational central bank independence to the Bank of England and its newly formed Monetary Policy Committee. There had been an enormous and influential research effort over the previous two decades devoted to understanding the case for the adoption of central bank independence. Much of this research had passed into received economic wisdom about the appropriate formulation of monetary policy. As explained in the previous chapter, it became clear that the absence of a credible commitment by the monetary authorities to price stability would induce a positive (and costly) bias to equilibrium inflation outcomes. An independent central bank with a credible commitment to price stability was widely thought to be the way to establish such credibility. This key debate was particularly instrumental in the United Kingdom. It provided the stimulus for a series of reforms to the monetary constitution of the United Kingdom in the 1990s, following the exit from the ERM in 1992, and culminated with the granting of operational independence for the Bank of England in 1997.[1]

Despite overwhelming theoretical evidence, the empirical evidence in the 1990s of the impact of operational central bank

---

[1] The next section draws heavily on Chadha, McMillan and Nolan, (2007).

independence had been limited, offering at best qualified support for the benefits of such a framework.[2] We were fortunate therefore that the incoming Labour government in the United Kingdom in 1997 decided to make a 'surprise' announcement about the creation of operational independence for the Bank of England on its fifth day of office. Although a decision to reform some aspects of the monetary constitution was expected, the crucial and final step of operational independence for the Bank of England was a surprise to the financial markets on the morning of 6 May 1997. We should further note that the announcement did neither entail any reduction in the central target for inflation nor any change in the measure of inflation. It involved a number of procedural changes, with the main force of the policy initiative being that of operational independence.[3] Ben Bernanke (2003) argued that 'the maintenance of price stability – and equally important, the development by the central bank of a strong reputation for and commitment to it – serves to anchor the private sector's expectations of future inflation'.

The decision to grant independence on that day was a surprise to the markets, many in H. M. Treasury and primarily to the Bank of England itself. In fact, the chancellor's decision to grant operational independence was only openly discussed with incoming Prime Minister Blair on polling day itself, 1 May 1997.[4] The Labour Party's Business Manifesto published on 11 April 1997 had proposed the

---

[2] The touchstone for this literature was Alberto Alesina and Lawrence Summer's (1993) finding of a negative association between the extent of central bank independence and low inflation but no significant relationship with output growth.

[3] Short-term policy rates were also raised by 25bp on 'Independence Day', but this move was widely expected and led to little or no movement in the short end of the yield curve; for example, in April 1997 a Goldman Sachs UK economics analyst reported that we expect a base rate rise of at least twenty-five basis points at the May monetary meeting and Paribas Economic Research produced a similar forecast on 7 April.

[4] Andrew Rawnsley (2000) used private interviews to establish this element of the surprise, page 3 and 31. Note that 5 May 1997 was a Bank Holiday Monday and so the decision was delayed to the Tuesday by this Public Holiday.

following reform to the Bank of England, which fell well short of operational independence:

> We propose a new monetary policy committee to decide on the advice which the Bank of England should give to the chancellor.[5]

In the week following the announcement, the newspaper *The Economist* actually complained that the reform was not signalled in the Labour Party manifesto and was not debated or discussed as a serious policy initiative.[6] This decision surprised everybody, including, many at the Bank of England and the Treasury.[7] Certainly, in subsequent interviews the officials at the Bank of England have admitted both market and personal surprise at the announcement. Howard Davies (2000), then deputy governor at the Bank of England, suggested in an interview that the announcement was to the market's surprise.

Governor Sir Eddie George also admitted in an interview that he was not expecting immediate operational independence and drew a link to the likely impact on longer-term interest rates:

> I was very surprised by the timing – the decision to move [on independence] immediately on taking office ... the markets believed that the politicians would not let go of the decisions on implementation of monetary policy. And this was damaging. It meant that inflation expectations did not adjust to the extent that they might have done to the decline in actual inflation. The impact on expectations is shown by the fact that bond yields dropped 50 basis points on the announcement by the incoming government in May 1997.[8]

With Peter McMillan and Charles Nolan (2007), I examined the consequence for longer-term interest rates, and found that inflation-

---

[5] Quoted by Denzil Davies (Labour) M. P. in Hansard on 11 November 1997, column 737.

[6] *The Economist*, 10 May 1997, page 13.

[7] William Keegan (2001) *The Observer*, 17 June 2001.

[8] Central Banking Publications Limited, 25 March 2002, page 22.

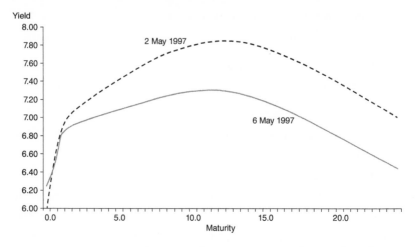

FIGURE 5.2 Long-term nominal interest rate pre-and post-independence

fighting preferences were highly likely to impact on interest rates and explained well the significant decrease in interest rates shown in Figure 5.2. A permanent fall of ½ per cent in borrowing costs means that for every £1bn borrowed or refinanced by the government since 1997, the state has saved some £5mn. I leave it to the reader to look at how much the government has borrowed in that period. The value of central bank independence looks clear – it can significantly reduce medium and long nominal rates for both government and private sector liabilities.

5.3   ASPECTS OF ECONOMIC PERFORMANCE

Far ahead, ten-year inflation expectations, as measured by the prices of conventional and (RPI) index-linked bonds, provide an indication of the extent to which it is believed that the policy regime will deliver stable inflation. We can see for the most part stable long-run inflation expectations from this source and surveys. Note that RPI inflation started to rise from 2005 onwards, in part as the result of house components and mortgage interest rate payments and this tended to drag up long-term RPI inflation expectations without necessarily indi-cating a loss of credibility. Indeed, if we examine other survey

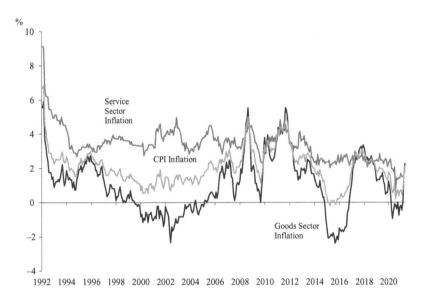

FIGURE 5.3 CPI inflation decomposed

measures of inflation expectations from this period, belief in the targets seemed to be sustained.

At the same time, the performance of CPI inflation seems to have been a tale of two sectors: services and goods. With increasing market penetration from the emerging world at lower finished goods prices, goods sector inflation became persistently negative in this period and played a role in explaining how relatively easy it was to maintain low inflation in this period. John Lewis and Jumana Saleheen (2016) estimate that switching to emerging market–sourced goods reduced manufactured import price inflation by just under 0.9 percentage points per annum on average, and overall import price inflation by around 0.6 percentage points per annum. Although part of the story for low inflation in this period also arises from the exchange rate and the increasing productivity of the distribution sector, as suggested by Steve Nickell in 2005, it is also quite possible that forward-looking agents were setting prices and mark-ups in line with the inflation target. So if the real side of the economy and the expected sequences of output gaps were in broad agreement with price stability, what about the monetary and financial sector, where there had been a considerable expansion in activity?

Michael McLeay and Ryland Thomas (2016) have shown that money and credit both grew faster than nominal GDP – the current value of all spending in the economy – throughout the long expansion (and during the decade before), and that credit grew faster than money. This kind of work provides a vital insight into the financial crisis of 2007, in that it was preceded by credit growth originating from wholesale, financial institutions, rather than household or retail funding of the banking system. These results are consistent with stories about a global savings glut, a narrowing of risk premia on a wide class of assets and a 'search for yield' that helped drive credit and housing bubbles prior to the US sub-prime crisis. In effect, the UK banks' 'customer funding gap' was filled by an abundance of funds channelled through the wholesale interbank market, much of which originated overseas, and these flows rapidly reversed when the interbank markets froze in 2007/2008 with the onset of the financial crisis. Alastair Milne and Justine Wood (2016) also have provided evidence of a substantial credit expansion, especially in lending secured on property. Yet they show that this led to only relatively modest losses for UK banks on residential mortgage lending in the crisis period of 2008–2013. Instead, losses in UK bank sterling lending were more closely associated with commercial property lending.

The global lowering of real interest rates resulted directly as a market-clearing response to the burgeoning savings in many emerging economies. Without access to external funds from emerging economies, the real or natural interest rate in the advanced economies would lie at point **a** in Figure 5.4. But when we add a pool of savings from countries with a greater desire to save at any given interest rate, we can then see how real rates in advanced economies fall from **a** to **c** and increase from **b** to **c** in newly industrialised economies when we add this large net supply of savings from overseas as part of the globalisation phenomenon. A new set of countries started to produce and trade and derived higher income but also tended to have a higher

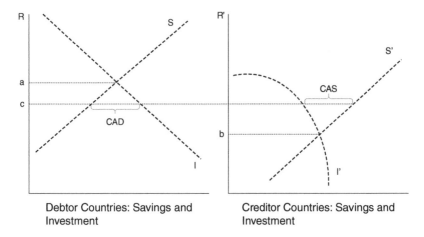

Debtor Countries: Savings and Investment

Creditor Countries: Savings and Investment

FIGURE 5.4 The Metzler diagram

propensity to save. In the language of central bankers, they were more risk-averse. This meant in the world as a whole, the savings schedule moved out and the markets of loanable funds cleared at a lower interest rate.

So real interest rates across the world have been pushed down along a secular trend in part by the integrating emerging economies. Countries in fast-growing economies with a tendency to save have recycled those savings abroad. This shift in real interest rates has contributed to the chronic UK current account deficit, where we buy more goods and services from overseas than we sell. But these real rates have also provided a considerable fillip to global asset prices but to the UK housing market, in particular, which has constraints on supply but for which demand has sharply increased alongside a reduction in borrowing costs. This has contributed to high levels of household and firm-level indebtedness that both stood at around 80 per cent of GDP, prior to the COVID-19 crisis.

In effect, the newly emergent economies, in a world with a shortage of risk-free assets, have behaved in a risk-averse manner, lending large volumes of funds to advanced economies, such as the United Kingdom, with long-lived credit histories and correspondingly deep financial markets. One way to look at the secular fall in rates, is that the resource base – measured by GDP – is become more domin-ated by these new economies rather than the more risk-loving bor-rowers in advanced economies. Hence, the world real interest rate has been declining as a larger fraction of world output is accounted for by risk-averse newly industrialised economies. The United Kingdom, therefore, by holding a positive net position in overseas equities and a negative net position in debt, is absorbing risk from the rest of the world, which it does not wish to carry. In effect, the United Kingdom has been borrowing from countries such as China, which are risk-averse, and using the proceeds to buy foreign equity and acting not a little like the very hedge funds it has dotted around Mayfair.

The sequences of current account deficits in the debtor coun-tries represent the same phenomenon, as the flows of capital from saver to debtor countries simply correspond to borrowing by debtor countries to buy goods and services: very much like running a bank overdraft with the bank lending you money. These now globally lower real interest rates raise the value of assets, which are exactly equal to the expected risk-adjusted cash flows over the life of any asset. If the real rate falls, so does the rate at which we discount the future, and indeed if risk falls, asset prices must also rise. Additionally for the main asset on any household's financial portfolio, which is the house in which it dwells, any net equity held by householders also provides a highly valuable source of liquidity in terms of collateral for loans against which temporary shocks to income can be smoothed.[9]

With significant flows from abroad, Tomas Key, Martin Weale and Tomaz Wieladek (2016) have explored one aspect of the international position at that time: how the United Kingdom was able, despite a current account trade deficit and apparent net external liabilities, both to earn a positive balance of net income from abroad almost every year and to improve its net external position during the Long Expansion. The puzzle is that the regular current account deficit, particularly in the ten

---

[9] Just to be clear, because it is a word that is used without a good definition, liquidity is simply the ability to turn an asset into cash or directly into consumption.

years leading up to the financial crisis, does not square with the stability of net external assets over that period, as we would expect liabilities (borrowing) to grow faster than assets (claims) unless there were higher systematic capital gains on the United Kingdom's assets compared with its liabilities. And, in fact, between 1997 and 2012 the United Kingdom seemed to have earned a total of capital gains or unidentified income worth nearly 20 per cent of 2012 GDP despite the fact that its net asset position is shown as a debtor. A substantial component of the improvement in the net income flow between the early 1990s and the middle of the subsequent decade appears to have been a consequence of regulatory changed in the UK's favour.

The overall picture that emerges is that inflation and its expectation was stable and this seemed to imply that there was macroeconomic stability at large. However, at precisely this moment in economic history – as possibly the unification of monetary beliefs provided some impetus to international trade amongst increasingly like-minded nations – there was a substantial deepening in globalisation that meant there was a deflation in imported goods, a persistent set of current account deficits in the advanced nations, lower real interest rates and an increasing compression in financial spreads. In this world, traditional monetary policy seemed to have nothing much to do, as inflation looked to be stable. But the risks, with higher levels of debt and an increasingly complex network of financial payoffs, were burgeoning like the iceberg under the water level or eyeline; and we were careering towards it.

5.3.1 Are Increases in House Prices Net Wealth?

Much of the activity in banking, credit and financial flows found its way into the UK housing market. We can note, in what we might term the parable of housing wealth, that during the Long Expansion, there was a tripling in the average UK house price. Whilst liabilities on dwellings continued to grow as the background to this expansion, much of the measured increase in total household wealth can be explained by the increase in residential wealth.

Yet it turns out that the increase in wealth might be more apparent than real. Imagine an individual who lives for three periods, who saves £50 per period. At the end of the first period, she buys a house for £100 of which £50 is her equity and £50 is a mortgage. In the first period of her life we can imagine she lives in her parent's home. In the final period of her life she sells her house for £100 and pays off her mortgage. At the end of the three periods she has accumulated £150 of wealth, which is the three periods of £50 of savings and actually does not sound very rational, but let us suppose her planned funeral is lavish.

Next consider in period 2, that another individual is born who also saves £50 in period 2 and seeks to buy the house from the older person in the third period; his equity and debt of £100 is simply a transfer to the first individual. What determines the house price? Well it ought to be something like the present value of the (imputed or actual) rents that will accrue to the owner of the house over its lifetime, which is a function of the risk-free rate, a risk premium and any expected growth in rents. So let us suppose, that an increase in rents and a fall in real interest rates imply that the house price doubles. If this doubling occurs between the second and third period, the older individual will be left with an additional £100 of wealth. They can have a more lavish funeral or donate their wealth to an academic institution (or an academic). But overall, is society better off, because the area has become gentrified? Examine the position of the young individual who now has to take on £100 more debt in order to meet the higher price. The increase in the house price is simply a transfer from the young to the old (in this case from male to female) or from those who are short (in need, and so on the demand side) housing to those who are long (in possession and so on the supply side). We can extend the number of families so that another is born in period 3 and then from that period on, we always have old, middle-aged and young individuals and we can think of the vertical line as a family and exchange between individuals that has no net implications for overall wealth, which is always simply a function of accumulated savings.

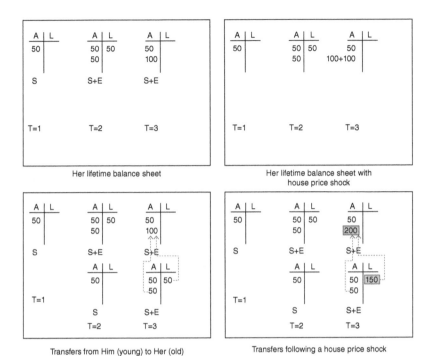

FIGURE 5.5 Transfers from young to old under house price appreciations

What is clear and stands, whether increases in house prices increases net wealth (permanent income) or not, is that the increase in house prices has been associated with an increase in the quantity of private sector financial claims and growth in both credit and debt. As two sides of the balance sheet they will sum to zero but leave each side of the balance sheet vulnerable to two quite distinct risks. The debtor may find themselves constrained if they reach their borrowing limit or if there are unexpected changes in interest rates or their income that make debt plans unsustainable. On the other hand, the creditor may face the prospects of default or unanticipated falls in the returns from savings, which would undermine his or her future expenditure plans. It is the size of these claims and their resulting fragility to all kinds of shocks in income, oil prices, interest rates or default, that made the economy vulnerable. Many central banks, however, were fixated on the parable of housing wealth rather than the risks arising from an increasingly fragile structure of payments and claims.

5.4 INFLATION TARGETING: FLEXIBLE, AUGMENTED NUTTERS?

As we have discussed earlier, the policy ineffectiveness proposal suggested that policy would have to be news, or unanticipated, if it was to influence the private sector's previously formulated plans. The surprise announcement of central bank independence would casually seem to be a natural extension of that form of reasoning. Indeed, some years later the surprise announcements about quantitative easing were carefully scrutinised for their impact on market expectations of future policy rates. On Independence Day in May 1997, there seemed to be a large downward shift in long-term rates, as market participants viewed the new regime as credible and more likely to stabilise inflation than an inflation targeter subject to political interference. Furthermore, it was argued by Mervyn King (1997) – prior to the adoption of operational independence – that the 'appropriate design of institutional arrangements (may) provide incentives for [a] central banker to pursue the first-best state-contingent policy' as he would wish to be judged on his performance against the target and would strive to hit the target and be prepared to explain any errors. We shall examine the merits of this claim and also consider the debate on whether central banks ought to have paid more attention to the evolution of asset prices in setting policy.

The dynamic inconsistency of optimal rules, discussed in the previous chapter, is all about understanding the changing incentives faced by policymakers. If it seems likely that the incentives for the policymaker to renege on previously announced rules, the private sector will act on that incentive rather than any policy statement, and so will lead to a bias in outcomes that will always frustrate policy objectives. It is in the end a call for institutional competence. Recall that although the monetary authorities have goals for output and inflation stabilisation, they may also have an incentive to raise output above its potential. Such an inflation bias can only be solved with a credible commitment technology that rules about this incentive: the gold standard, as discussed in Chapter 1, provided a pretty good example. Under a gold standard the central bank's note issuance, a liability, was convertible to gold. This asset was held in limited supply and so excessive note issue would threaten bankruptcy of the central bank. The governor of a central bank who would want the institution to remain in existence would simply not have an option to increase note issuance beyond a credible level of backing or support. Such was the longevity and success of this technology, that we still aim for the metaphorical objective of a gold standard in so many aspects of public policy, from A-levels or health care. The monetary solution to this problem for a fiat money world was suggested by Carl Walsh (1995), who suggested linking a financial penalty on the central bank or its governor(s) that was equivalent to the public's calculation of any inflation bias. One obvious way to do that would be to set salaries and pensions in line with the CPI target and not link them to CPI outturns and ensure that misses in inflation on either side would be subtracted from income. However, such a tight target might induce central banks to behave in Mervyn King's memorable classification, as inflation 'nutters' who do not respond sufficiently to output shocks, a point to which we shall return.

The alternative would be to appoint a central banker in the spirit of Ken Rogoff (1985), who does not offer a full commitment technology but is known to have strong anti-inflation preferences. In this world, such a central banker offers a better inflation stabilisation option than discretion or, say it loud and proud or quietly, a politician, but in this case, at the cost of a less flexible response to other types of shocks, supply or asset price or otherwise. Such a conservative central banker is preferable to both one wishing to work by simple discretion, where inflation pinned down by private sector expectations and not actually 'controlled' or set by the policymaker, and the world where she is an inflation or employment 'nutter'. In this latter case where either one objective dominates the other, it tends to lead to higher welfare losses when measured in terms of variances in both inflation and output. However, even this solution is not better than what can be described as the optimal state contingent policy, which eliminates the inflation bias and lowers output volatility to its primitive level. The phrase – optimal state contingent policy – is cumbersome but simply implies that the policymaker can be trusted by private sector agents to act on shocks in such a manner all the time and with regard to their long-run reputation or the historical judgement of their actions that are in line with the social optimum. Such a policy has been termed 'timeless' by Mike Woodford (2005) and by many central bankers as a fair reflection of what they seek to do on behalf of society; as custodians of the social norm of price stability, the Money Minders.

It has been argued that an inflation target with transparent monitoring rather than simply being about appointing a conservative central banker actually helps implement the optimal policy. This is because it simply imposes some cost of missing the inflation target through public embarrassment: does the governor want to sit in the press conference and bow his or her head at the appropriate angle and for the appropriate length of time in apology? Or should we impose financial costs to ensure good central bank behaviour via some elaborate clawback of salary and pensions in the event of inflation targets being missed? Rather, it was felt that the inflation targeting under operational independence would allow people to assess ex post outcomes relative to ex ante targets that would act to tie the hands of policymakers to the target over time and prevent any dynamic inconsistency. Central bankers do want to be respected by their peers, when they go to Jackson Hole or Sintra on their bus drivers' holidays.

This emphasis on the link between expectations and outcomes placed considerable weight on the need for central bank communication and transparency, superficially, so that plans and outcomes could be clearly assessed. More subtly it was also a way of 'controlling' forward-looking agents so that targets became easier to hit. Consider a forward-looking agent deciding on wage demands, price setting and the composition of their asset holdings. If such a person believes (has credibility) in the inflation target and understands what policy responses will be implemented in response to various states of nature that are expected with some probability but not yet revealed, they can make plans that are consistent with the inflation target.

In fact, a parallel debate even started about whether inflation targets were really optimal because it could be that a target for the price level itself, rather than its rates of change, might be a clearer path for forward planning and contracting, so that agents would know what the CPI index number would be well into the future. Inflation is simply about stabilising the change in the price level and if there are occasionally larger or smaller changes in the price level we let bygones be bygones, which means that looking to the very long run we do not know what the exact price index number will be: controlling the rate of drift in a ship may not get you exactly to the port of your destination, it was argued. A price level target would allow us to expect that the price level of 100 in today's terms would be 110 in 2025 or 120 in 2030, and to plan with a greater degree of precision. It was also argued that because we had pinned down the actual price level so far in advance, in the event of any large downward shock where, for example, today's price level falls to 95 – in the case of credibility – we would actually start to expect a return back to the normal path and more rapid price rises than if a strict inflation target was maintained. It was probably at this point that we started to over-engineer the solution to the problem of ensuring price stability![10]

Even the arguments on the need for transparency went further. If agents understood the policy target and the responses of the central bank to various states, which is called the reaction function, then actual policy decisions need no longer be a surprise to be effective, as they will already have been factored into decisions made by private agents. So policy effectiveness seemed to have been turned on its head

---

[10] And the Federal Reserve did indeed move to a flexible average inflation framework in August 2020. See Powell's Jackson Hole address, "New Economic Challenges and the Fed's Monetary Policy Review".

with the normal stream of policy meetings and choices thought to have been more effective if they had no 'surprise' element. These arguments were taken to extreme levels by some analyses of policy-making by the FOMC, which showed very little surprise element from futures contracts based on the Federal Funds rate (John Carlson et al., 2006). There was perhaps a further consequence of this fall in the uncertainty attached to policy rates that the funding costs of financial intermediation were not only low but also did not engender any great risk in terms of their variance over time: in funding costs what you expected is what you seem to get always and other prices do simply not behave that way in response to changing circumstances. The apogee of this approach was when the FOMC raised the Federal Funds rate in twenty-five basis point steps over seventeen consecutive meetings from 2004 to 2006 with none acting to surprise the markets. With hindsight, it might have been better not to have attempted to over-engineer an artificial degree of certainty in the path of policy rates, as there is always some uncertainty about the world that is yet to be resolved. And, of course, something that may seem to have been resolved may once again become uncertain.

The real debate on policy in this period was between those who thought that even inflation targeters should 'lean against the wind' of asset price changes and those who felt that inflation targeting, perhaps with some flexibility, was a sufficient policy. Many have outlined the basic response to asset price fluctuations in an inflation-targeting world. Financial factors, including asset prices, matter for the formulation of monetary policy in so far as they provide information for current and future capacity utilisation and consequently inflationary pressures. Furthermore, a compression in financial spreads and other market-determined interest rates could be thought of as an increase in the neutral policy rate. The feedbacks are interesting. As financial risks accumulated with higher levels of debt, the economy-wide neutral rate may fall further and also may have more limited room to move in a more sensitive indebted economy that is highly sensitive to interest rate changes. Accordingly, changes in the financial structure may alter the natural rate of interest rate and the optimal monetary policy strategy or reaction function. In various applications of models in which an external finance premia affected monetary conditions, it was generally found that it was not necessary to target asset prices in order to locate a more stable or preferable equilibrium. Part of the reason is that in the real world, of course, asset prices are likely to be conditioned on a forecast of policy itself and so targeting may even reduce the efficacy of policy: think of putting your feet on the accelerator and brake of your car at the same time.

Responding directly to asset prices was rather tricky: was it a fundamental asset price change or a bubble? I still place little trust in anyone who tries to tell me in real time about any asset price change being one or the other; we simply do not know.

This means that we might be responding to perfectly valid reappraisals of the value of an asset based on the present value of its returns. Even if we were sure that there was an asset boom and we raised rates to offset the boom there would be two further problems. First, how much would we have to raise policy rates by to reduce asset prices and to what extent will these rate rises be costly in terms of output losses? Secondly, the resultant crash in asset prices will require a rapid fall in rates while the previous impetus from rate rises is still working its way through the monetary transmission mechanism and policy will once again be acting as brake and accelerator, which is not a good thing. Charlie Bean (2003) argues that the best response is not to try and offset the credit boom while it is happening, that 'the optimal policy is in effect to ignore the asset boom, but to mitigate the fallout when it collapses. Furthermore the expectation of a looser monetary policy in the event of a future credit crunch raises expected inflation. Consequently there is an upward bias to inflation'. Obviously the model developed was not to be taken literally, but the idea that a credit boom and bust was best left to be cleared up after the fact was certainly the dominant monetary policy parable.

Lars Svensson (2009), in his survey of how the financial crisis impacted on the operation of flexible inflation targeting, thinks that

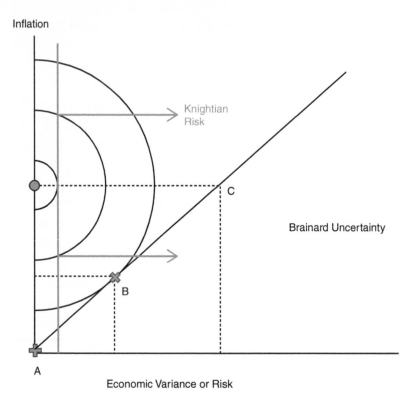

FIGURE 5.6 Why an inflation undershoot can make sense

little has changed. That is not to argue financial factors are not important. Financial factors can be thought to impact in quite an important way on the monetary transmission mechanism – that is how policy rates impact on the real economy – and need to be carefully studied to ensure that all information from them are incorporated in the policy stance. Indeed even prior to the crisis, it was felt that financial stability might be thought of as an occasionally binding constraint on monetary policy – which meant that if and when a crisis emerged, monetary policy may end up being constrained while the crisis was being cleaned up; yet most of the time these issues could then be ignored. Such an approach may mean that we have to lengthen the horizon over which interest rate policy aims to get the economy back to normal and plan over ever-longer horizons: a kind of smoothing result, which economists and central bankers do tend to like. Even directly responding to asset prices could be assumed to fit in with a need to ensure stability in capacity utilisation over the long run, if we could extract the signals about demand and supply from their often volatile movements.

We can translate some of these ideas and revisit our analysis from the previous chapter with the help of Bill Brainard's analysis. As well as outcomes in terms of inflation on the vertical axis, we have economic risk on the horizontal axis. There is Bliss Point to the North of [A], where inflation is at target and there is no uncertainty. Each concentric circle maps an equal point of indifference, but circles nearer the Bliss Point are preferred. If the economy starts at Point [A], the policymaker must decide where to drive the economy. The first observation is that with inflation below target, she will be looking to inject some demand if feasible and not too dangerous, by which I mean likely to stoke up some induced economic volatility. The line [ABC] traces the constraint facing this policymaker because when she tries to inject more demand into the economy she cannot be sure of the economy's response, and so there is more uncertainty to be faced. Even though point [C] would eliminate the inflation losses, point [B] is to be preferred, because she prefers less uncertainty to being closer to the target along the trade-off curve or constraint. This economy ends up with a bit more macroeconomic uncertainty and an undershoot in inflation and is where some people think the economy ought to have been during the Long Expansion, that is, with tighter monetary policy and somewhat lower inflation. It is possible to think of the economy in the Long Expansion as having moved to point [C], where there were no inflation losses but economic and financial uncertainties were building up and not especially well measured. The parable of the conservative central banker was reborn.

Indeed it might be possible to get the same kind of result if the policymaker only cared about inflation and did not agree to having uncertainty in their calculation of welfare. This is a policymaker who acts in what is called a certainty equivalent manner – where risk does not militate against decisions. In this case the indifference curves would be horizontal lines and the policymaker would go directly to the Bliss Point – perhaps with some hubris – and state that they had maximised rather than traded off some welfare and ended boom and bust. Finally, the policymaker may think that they did not bring about any increase in economic risk as a result of their own policy but that it was quite a separate matter from monetary policy. In this world the policymaker will think that they have arrived at the Bliss Point unmeasured or ignored or, that what we typically term, Knightian risk, after Frank Knight, is driving the economy to increasingly bad equilibria, and this is shown as the vertical feasible line shifting out to the right. With inflation broadly on target but (financial) risk severely underestimated by policymakers (see, for example, an evidence note from Alan Clarke, Paul Mortimer-Lee and myself, 2007), we arrived in a position where the economy seemed to be on track but lay on a fragile foundation. The gaps between perception and reality may be quite large, take some time to iron themselves out and also drive economic fluctuations while they do so.

5.5   MONEY AND THE MODELS

Although there is widespread agreement that in the long run there is, more or less, a one-to-one relationship between money growth and inflation and no relationship between money growth and real quantities, there is little consensus on the relationship, if any, between money and shorter-run economic developments. So the role monetary aggregates might play in the conduct of monetary policy in the short run in cases where money, its components or the interest rates at which various money markets clear, might give a varying degree of guidance to short-run movements in output and inflation. In this respect the European Central Bank has typically followed a two-pillar approach. It is argued that the first of these pillars gives a prominent role, a 'broadly based assessment of the outlook for future price developments' and economic analysis, and shock and the second pillar relies on a monetary analysis of trends (Stark, 2008). By contrast, the

Federal Reserve has in the past explicitly eschewed any role for money in the conduct of monetary policy. The Bank of England has also placed a less prominent weight on money, not least because financial liberalisation and changing payment technologies have masked the inflationary signal from growth in observed money aggregates.[11]

At the same time, the role of banks, other financial institutions and the financial system – that provide loans and help determine asset prices – are often given particular prominence in discussions on the transmission mechanism of monetary policy.[12] Therefore, a significant corpus of economists have not given up entirely on the idea that the monetary aggregates can sometimes contain information about the future state of the economy, as well as about the transmission mechanism of monetary policy, and may help identify risks to the economic outlook. To borrow an analogy from Nobu Kiyotaki and John Moore (2001) 'the flow of money and private securities through the economy is analogous to the flow of blood ... money is the blood that dispatches resources in response to those (price) signals' (p. 5).

More recently, and especially in light of seemingly every present turbulence in world financial markets, economists have been re-examining the role that money, and more generally credit, can play independently of the policy rate. One avenue that has been explored is motivated by the role of money or credit as a supply of payment services to credit-constrained consumers. The price, as a premium above the policy rate, of such loans, reflects the marginal costs to banks of their supply, and so it responds to increases in the efficiency of supply relative to the demand for loans. This relative price can move out of line with the policy rate set by the central bank when there are independent sources of fluctuations in the ability of financial intermediaries to supply credit or liquidity, for example, as a result of their efficiency in screening loans (monitoring) or the value of posted collateral. The understanding of this

[11] Woodford (2007) and King (2002).
[12] See Bernanke et al. (1999) for a clear exposition.

separate avenue of transmission provides motivation for a whole new class of policies: forget the policy rate and act on financial spreads.

Understanding the role of money and credit in judging economic fluctuations may even lead to more use of money as the instrument. Following the financial crisis, central banks used central bank money, or at least central bank liabilities, extensively as an additional instrument of monetary policy, which fitted well with a need to augment interest rate policy if it were substantially constrained at the zero lower bound or indeed simply had to deal directly with a malfunctioning financial system that otherwise had shifted the supply curve for money and its counterparts too far to the left, disrupting the availability of money and credit. The new instrument of central bank balance sheets fits very well into the development of game theoretic nostra for central bankers. This is because complementary instruments may well augment the signalling impact of both the current level of interest rates and the expected path of interest rates. Note that one popular solution to the problem of controlling a forward-looking system of rational agents is to make it easier for those agents to forecast future policy, and so condition their plans in line with the policymaker's objectives.[13] Thus, any strategy that is consistent with signalling that interest rates will be low for a long period may help reduce real rates over a longer horizon and raise price level expectations away from a deflationary pull.

5.5.1   Money Matters

As we have examined before, the long-run neutrality of money with respect to the real economy is a central plank of monetary policy making (Lucas, 1995). Although it is quite a simple matter to find long-run non-neutralities in many now-standard New Keynesian models, it is also generally accepted that long-run non-neutralities should not be exploited, as there is no clear enhancement in the welfare of the representative household. However, if we place aside

---

[13] See Woodford (2005).

the long-run or steady-state, day-to-day or month-to-month perturbations in the money market, this will lead to temporary changes in the market-clearing level of (overnight or short-term) money market rates and, because of various forms of informational uncertainty or indeed structural rigidity, may lead to temporary deviations in the expected real rate from its natural level, and thus act on aggregate demand. The key question is the extent to which shocks emanating from the money markets, and more broadly the markets for financial assets and claims, can be stabilised by an interest rate rule or indeed whether an additional tool may required.[14]

We have already examined the seminal analysis of this question by Bill Poole (1970), who took a standard IS-LM framework and analysed the impact on output variance from setting either interest rates or the money supply in the presence of stochastic shocks to either or both of spending or money market equations. He showed that, in general, neither instrument would necessarily stabilise the economy better then the other as it depended on the relative magnitude of shocks in these sectors and the sensitivity of output to these respective shocks. An often overlooked implication of his analysis was that in general, some use of both instruments was likely to stabilise the output better than one instrument alone, a point to which we shall return, but one that is perhaps echoed by the experience of policymakers worldwide as they have had to augment interest rate tools' direct expansion of the central bank balance sheet.

The central bankers' central bank, the Bank for International Settlements (BIS), from a disinterested position, did not have to set monetary policy and regularly expressed concern about what we might call a worrying triplet. This triplet comprises high internal and external debt levels, high asset prices and rapidly growing broad money aggregates. William White (2009) added to worries about whether it was sensible to partition monetary and financial issues with a further concern: the horizon over which policy sought to

---

[14] See Chadha et al. (2014) on this point.

stabilise that was also part of the problem. 'Central banks have put too much emphasis on achieving near term price stability' (p. 2) at the expense of considering in detail what the implications may be for longer-run macroeconomic stability coming from the build-up in domestic and international 'imbalances'. Of course, central banks have explored the notion of flexible inflation targeting, where, financial considerations may operate as an occasionally binding constraint which would, in principle extend or contract the horizon over which inflation would be brought back to target. But who wants to attend the IMF annual meetings having just missed their inflation target?

Any direct discussion of a special role for financial intermediation leads us to reconsider, in the first instance, the relevance of Ben Bernanke and Alan Blinder's (1988) model of credit and demand. In comparison with the two asset world of the LM curve where there is simply a choice between money and bonds, if credit is not a perfect substitute for bonds then the quantity of loans and the external finance premium will matter for the determination of macroeconomic equilibrium. In other words, the spending equation will be not only determined by the single interest rate that ensures equilibrium in the money market but also the interest rates in the broader credit (or loan) markets, and so it is the allocation of funds across narrow and broad money by financial institutions which will matter for the level of aggregate demand.

This important point was mostly neglected in the first part of the great DSGE (micro-founded macroeconomics) revolution of monetary policymaking that took place over the subsequent two decades, in which the Modigliani-Miller theorem held continual sway as issues about the structure of the real economy's price rigidities and the correct monetary policy strategy took centre stage, with financial intermediation and monetary quantities having no special role to play in explaining the current level and likely path of the short-term policy rate.[15] Money was

---

[15] Two big ideas here. One relates to the four-letter acronym of DSGE, which literally stands for dynamic stochastic general equilibrium model but signifies an agenda that is searching for macroeconomic models that respect the Lucas Critique and so can be used for policy analysis by welfare criteria. The second is Modigliani-Miller

not only neutral and played no direct role in the equilibrium outcomes studied by monetary theorists but was actually just pinned down by optimal real choices and so did not even have any information content.

From the policy perspective the prosaic answer of the Bundesbank and, latterly, of the ECB is that money does indeed matter. It is broad money growth that is associated one for one with growth in nominal expenditure and that timely and accurate analysis of monetary dynamics constitutes (arguably) the most important part of the central bank's information set. Indeed, Mervyn King (2002), the soon-to-be governor of the Bank of England, in a paper written while he was deputy governor, argues that money is important because it is an imperfect substitute for a wide variety of assets and so a change in its quantity will induce some rebalancing of financial portfolios and impact on nominal demand with both direct effects on real assets and indirect effects, as financial yields will change. In other words, the yields from many financial assets may enter the broad money demand function and with some prescience, he contends that money may matter simply because it relaxes transaction costs and promotes liquidity, a point taken up by many academics subsequently and Tobin previously.

As pointed out by Charles Goodhart (2007) and Nobu Kiyotaki and John Moore (2001), money (aggregates) should be made to matter in general equilibrium models as they affect consumption decisions of liquidity constrained households and the spreads across several financial instruments and assets. And Mike Woodford (2007) states 'money matters' in such circumstances as it may be the root of disequilibrium and instability in the economy originating from the financial sector.

The quantity of money plays little or no active role in many latter-day macroeconomic models, in which money tends to be pinned down exactly by plans formulated by households and firms for demand and production, which then determine output and

which simply states that the value of a firm is not affected by whether it uses debt or equity to finance its expenditures and so disallows the notion of financial frictions leading to a preference for one type or the other.

inflation outcomes directly. In this sense the money stock does not appear to provide any independent source of macroeconomic fluctuations. Typically, it is the price of money, the short-term policy rate, that regulates aggregate demand and is used as the instrument of monetary policy, with money supplied elastically to meet any idiosyncratic money market shocks. In such models the policy interest rate is sufficient to determine the constellation of market interest rates, and money (or credit) exerts no independent effect on the economy, via these other interest rates, and so becomes less worthy of study (Goodhart, 2007). Accordingly, current monetary policy practice is somewhat ambivalent about the role of monetary aggregates. Indeed it is worth rereading some evidence submitted to the Treasury Committee in 2007 under their enquiry into Ten Years of the MPC:

> One ongoing concern is the absence of money or liquidity from the current generation of macroeconomic models. There is probably more agreement in practice over the use of money than it appears. As with a good trader, monetary policy makers should seek to exploit all available and robust correlations with the objects of primary interest. The trader will be concerned with the prices of assets on his or her book and the central banker with fluctuations in output and inflation. There are a number of reasons why a monetary policy maker should not, and in practice probably does not, ignore measures of monetary aggregates when setting monetary policy.

First, money may well provide an early real-time, albeit noisy, signal to the monetary policymaker about the state of the economy. Even though in the fullness of time the information from output and inflation may encompass the news from money, for those who have to make decisions in real time, many indicators, including money, may have valuable information. Secondly, the components of broad money are likely to provide some clues as to the extent to which financial frictions and collateral constraints are being altered by lending practices and whether the economic cycle is being amplified.

Finally, some fundamental aspects of the monetary balance sheet may require the central bank to monitor developments with monetary implications; for example, monetary and fiscal policies are tied via the government's budget constraint and imply a commitment by the fiscal authority to stabilise the level of public debt as a requirement of monetary stability. In this respect, I would encourage the continuation of the use of a clear long-term framework within which fiscal policy operates. Finally, the implications of developments in our measures of money may not fully reflect the impact of liquidity provision elsewhere on domestic markets (through carry trades) nor on the quantum of risk being run in domestic financial markets (e.g. due to an increased role for hedge funds) – so I would call for more work to measure monetary dynamics.

5.6   MATERIAL RISK

The noughties (or too temptingly the naughties) provided quite a party for the financial markets. The long economic expansion increased the probability of a bust but was supported in its longevity by the widely accepted falsehood that the probability of a bust had permanently fallen. It was a Titanic error. Perhaps we had discovered the secret of growth without limit or without a sudden stop; or perhaps, as some baby boomers were thinking: life without death. The inflation-targeting regime had offered a route towards locating something fairly close to an optimal rule. Central bankers could provide descriptions and explanations of what they did that might act to tie their hands; or perhaps they would always do the right thing, ignore political suasion and just 'get on with' securing price stability. Any siren voices that seem to have become noisier after the events were not very loud and like Gogol's Poprishchin, they can now be heard complaining that: 'They don't listen to me, they don't hear me, they don't see me.'

Agents could understand, even perhaps having been taught by past, current or future central bankers, why policymakers did what they did. And the interest rate reaction function when specified in terms of responses to inflation and output could not only be widely and easily understood but deviations in exact responses or the horizon over which targets would be met, could be thought of as ways to generate extra degrees of freedom in order to deal with off-model judgements and events related to increasingly obvious levels of financial fragility. Policymakers were not complacent and thought hard about how to deal with the consequence of financial bubbles and their bursting but did not perhaps understand the extent to which the Long Expansion had itself created a sense of invincibility and allowed risks to escalate to such an extent that the foundations of the economy has become unhinged. The events of August 2007 and over the next year quickly brought that sense of invincibility to an end.

6   The New Art of Central Banking

*In which the compact world of the central banker partitioned from
society and operating surgically in the pursuit of price stability become
more complex. And merges back into the domain of financial market
stabilisation, debt management, banking supervision, prudential
lending, asymmetries of risk. The host of interactions will have to lead to
a re-writing of institutional objectives and the framework of
macroeconomic policy-making. If it all falls on the Money Minders,
central banks will fail.*

She had a great many opinions, but taken together they did not add up to a
point of view.

V. S. Naipaul, Guerrillas, 1975

6.1   CONFRONTING RISKS

Without doubt, money and monetary policymaking has evolved
significantly. The original function of money was to allow trade with
a standardised unit of account. A monetary policy would originally
have implied simply some arrangement of institutional practice so
that the right amount of commodity-based money could be used to
facilitate the level of trade. It is probably the case, as is still the case
in many parts of the world, that large amounts of trade stood outside
the monetary system and relied on barter or non-pecuniary grace and
favours. Even standardisation was and remains no easy matter as it is
no simple task to set the correct relative prices between various
types of monies and goods, ensure the absence of counterfeiting, or
clipping, and decide on how to get the right amount of money into
circulation. We continue to debate whether notes should be limited
in denomination and whether monetary policy will have to be
rethought once all money is electronic, which is now part of the
very near future.

The experiences of the late eighteenth and nineteenth centuries
involved both a recognition that the rate of exchange of money for

gold might be changed in the event of crises but also that the banking and financial system required regular bouts of support because of a fragility inherent from the very nature of its operation. The guiding principles were framed by Bagehot and the evolution of monetary orthodoxy, or sound money, was evident. This orthodoxy suggested some adherence to low levels of public debt in peacetime, a gold standard and circumspect choice in the policy rate. The suspension of the gold standard associated with World War I, the interwar boom and bust and the Great Depression provided an incentive and a 'Keynes-inspired' blueprint for the operation of countercyclical monetary and fiscal policy.

While it is not entirely clear even now whether these policies were responsible for the economic recovery prior to World War II, it is clear that there had been a profound change in the responsibilities of government. Ralph Hawtrey (1932) summed up the interwar mood well:

> [T]he result has been not merely that the world has been insufficiently prepared to deal with the new problems of Central Banking which have arisen in the years since the War, but that it has failed even to attain the standard of wisdom and foresight that prevailed in the nineteenth century. Moreover, they should endeavour to adapt their measures of credit regulation, as far as their domestic position permits, to any tendency towards an undue change in the state of general business activity. An expansion of general business activity of a kind which clearly cannot be permanently maintained should lead Central Banks to introduce a bias towards credit restriction into the credit policy which they think fit to adopt, having regard to internal conditions in their own countries. On the other hand, an undue decline in general business activity in the world at large should lead them to introduce a bias towards relaxation. In pursuing such a policy the Central Banks will have done what is in their power to reduce fluctuations in business activity.

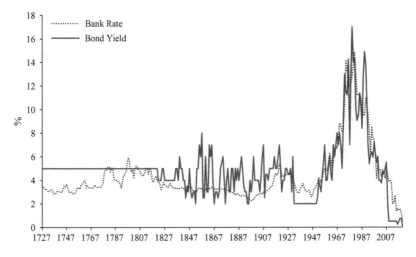

FIGURE 6.1 Bank Rate and long-term rates, 1727–2020

From that point on the rate of inflation and economic growth would continue to be the government's problem and an important back-drop to the assessment of the performance of political leadership – which at some level is rather odd given that the dominant models of economic fluctuations do not predict a permanent impact on output from monetary policy. As Figure 6.1 shows, monetary policy as tracked by Bank Rate seems to have become more active over time both in the level and the frequency of its changes. Note also the close relationship between bank rate and a long-term interest rate, in this case, on UK bonds where the latter looks very much like a moving average of the former, mostly.

Accordingly, in the post-war period, there was an incredible intellectual effort to understand not only the mechanical interplay between monetary policy and the real economy, via its impact on market interest rates and asset prices, but also how monetary policy effectiveness was a function of its interplay with private agents' plans and expectations. The elegant models developed allowed the study of optimal monetary policy and the development of strategies to minim-ise inefficient fluctuations in output, particularly in the aftermath of the end of Bretton Woods and the subsequent costly inflation and disinflation. The great mirage of the Long Expansion was that whilst it appeared that business cycle risks had been eliminated, they were, in fact, increasing rapidly. Once the risks became apparent, the economy quickly jumped to a world of profound financial constraints that acted to bear down on activity in a persistent manner. Interest rates hit the lower zero bound and public debt was stoked up to precarious levels for peacetime.

Practically speaking two issues were then exposed, which have occupied much of the debate on the setting of monetary policy. How should policymakers deal with a response to large, negative economic shocks that seemed to threaten to exhaust policy ammunition? What kind of defences should be put up so that such shocks could not build up in the same way, or that stocks of policy ammunition would still be available? The former problem led to the rediscovery of open market operations as a way of influencing longer-term interest rates.[1] These operations involve the central bank buying or selling bonds, typically issued by the government, from the private sector in exchange for central bank money in order to alter the maturity of private sector holdings of public debt. The latter problem led to the rediscovery of tools that act to constrain, or if you prefer place safe limits on, financial intermediation by requiring more holdings of reserves and capital.

However, there is another issue that has become more relevant. As well as thinking in terms of normal times – with small changes from the steady-state – and abnormal times as the world we are now in, with low growth in the period since the financial crisis as well as extraordinary policies, it is becoming increasingly clear that there is a

---

[1] For what follows, it is worth spelling out that a bond price is the present value of the interest payments and principal owed to the holder of the bond by the issuer. The present value calculation incorporates an interest rate forecast over the life of the bond and the price increases as interest rates fall because the present value of far-off payments is correspondingly higher. Thus, bond prices and interest rates move in opposite directions.

transitional state to work through. Debt does not disappear, default notwithstanding, overnight, and so balance sheet repair is a tricky and time-consuming business. Public debt will at best take decades to get back to pre-crisis levels and financial intermediaries may eventually start to allocate capital to the most productive firms, but at the same time, policy has to deal with nursing a sick economy rather than licking a healthy one into shape.

In this chapter, we will examine the main central bank policy lever used in the financial crisis: quantitative easing. We shall go on to examine the burgeoning central bank role for what have been called macroprudential instruments. The case for considering the policy nexus as some point in monetary-financial-fiscal space is still being explored but, in this triplet, lies a generalised way of thinking about policy and its transmission. I will then start to explore the need for further communication in order to guide people on possible central bank actions but also perhaps to elicit more information from people's private views. Finally, I conclude by considering the money minders one last time.

6.2   QUANTITATIVE EASING

When policy rates hit their effective lower bound of near zero, central banks were forced to consider how they might impact on market interest rates that typically followed movements in Bank Rate quite closely. These market interest rates form part of what central bankers call the monetary transmission mechanism and typically include short-term money market rates that forecast Bank Rate for one to three months, as well as government bonds of varying maturities. As we have already seen, the long-term bond rate is essentially a moving average of current and expected short-term Bank Rate and so if market participants could be persuaded that policy rates would stay at low levels for a long time, then these long-term rates would fall and provide some succour to an economy in a financial or deep economic crisis. One way to persuade market participants is to talk a lot, what is sometimes called 'open mouth operations', and so central banks try to persuade that they will 'do what it takes' to stabilise the economy,

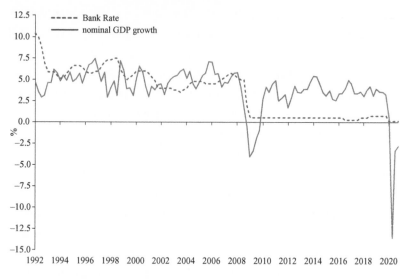

FIGURE 6.2 Policy rates and nominal GDP growth

which can be an effective strategy if credible, as the President of the ECB discovered in the summer of 2012; many central bankers echoed his words in 2020. When the economy hits a nadir something needs to be done and more importantly, needs to be seen to be done. One metric of the problem in 2008 was the large fall in the nominal GDP growth below Bank Rate. Nominal GDP is the sum of real output growth and inflation and Bank Rate sums a real rate and short-run inflation expectations, with both rates in normal times basically expected to be something like 4–5 per cent. In Figure 6.2 it is the large triangles below the policy rate in 2008 and 2009 and again in 2020 that created the motivation for QE, as a way of reducing emergent output gaps.

The signalling game can go quite far, and we have returned repeatedly to it, but central banks found that actual purchases of assets were required, which lowered long-term interest rates by one of two mechanisms. The first is that following a large increase in fiscal deficits, which acts to stimulate demand, market clearing in the money market will require higher interest rates in order to choke off some speculative money balances and allows the deployment of some money for transactions instead. Any increase in rates will tend to reduce the impact of the fiscal expansion. If on the other hand, money for transactions is expanded by some type of QE, interest rates need not rise and the full force of the stabilising effort will reach the economy.

The second is more subtle and relies on the argument that in buying bonds, which are high in price at a low interest rate, the central bank is signalling that it will not raise interest rates which would lead to an immediate lowering of bond prices and a, perhaps significant, loss on the trading operation. Personally, I put more weight on the former as central banks seem more likely than not to make money from these trades because they were providing market participants with much-needed liquidity in the form of central bank money in exchange for less liquid bonds and thus will be profitable over the whole sequence of operations involving purchase and eventual run-off.[2] Following the financial crisis of 2008, quantitative easing (QE) – which I define as large-scale purchases of financial assets in return for central bank reserves – became a key element of monetary policy for a number of major central banks whose interest rates were at, or close to, the zero lower bound. However, despite its widespread use, the question of the effectiveness of QE remains highly controversial, with many arguing that it is printing money and likely ultimately to be inflationary. But to the extent that there has been undermining of confidence in the nation's currency, the demand has remained stable and there has been no jump in the velocity of circulation. As long as that persists, a new tool seems to have been uncovered.

6.2.1 QE as an Open Market Operation

Generally speaking, quantitative easing is really just an extended open market operation involving the unsterilised swap of central bank money for privately held assets. Let me break up these ideas. An open market operation involves the swap of central bank money (a liability

---

[2] See my paper with Philip Turner and Bill Allen (2021) on how we might move from quantitative easing to tightening by changing the maturity mix on both sides of the central bank balance sheet and essentially reverse the operations in baby steps.

on its balance sheet) for the purchase of an asset. If the operation is sterilised, the resulting increase in central bank money is mopped up by the sale of some other asset on the central bank balance sheet, which means that the central bank money is retuned to the central bank, so that the overall impact is a change in the type of asset held. If, on the other hand, the supply of new central bank money is not immediately mopped up by further asset sales by the central bank then the market operation is said to be unsterilised and thus adds to the quantity of money in the economy, until it is reversed.

The key innovation that QE represents, and is quite separate from a short-term open market operation, is that the duration of the swap is intended to be both long term and for an uncertain time. As explained, an open market operation, if unsterilised, leads to an increase in the quantity of base, or outside money.[3] This money represents claims on the public sector and will not be neutral – by which I mean there will be an economic impact – with respect to any given expenditure plans if there is a real balance effect that induces a fall in interest rates. This is because the increase in money changes the price of claims on the public sector. If, however, the private sector fully discounts the present value of taxes that will need to be paid to meet these obligations, then these bonds will not represent net wealth and the operation may yet be neutral. The debate on the efficacy of such operations hinged on the question of whether the supply of outside money changed the wealth position of the private sector (see Gale, 1982).

The analysis of such operations lay outside the remit of the workhorse New Keynesian (NK) Model in which the evolution of monetary aggregates, which were simply a veil by which real planned transactions were effected, provided no additional feedback to the state of the economy. As explained, these models are highly tractable and were used to develop simple, precise policy prescriptions, even at

---

[3] Inside money represents claims from one part of the private sector to another but outside money is a claim of the private sector on the public sector and is a net asset.

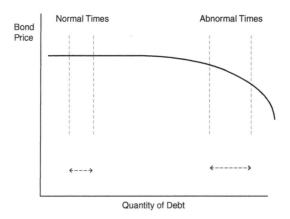

FIGURE 6.3 Bond prices and net supply

the lower zero bound of Bank Rate, by influencing expectations of the duration of any given level of Bank Rate in order to induce exchange rate depreciations or positive inflation shocks, and thus close any given sequence of output gaps in expectation. In these models, open market operations were neutral because at the lower zero bound money and bonds become perfect substitutes and any swap of one for the other does not change the wealth position of the private sector. In fact, in these models, QE-type policies are simply forms of commitment strategies that provide signals about the long-term intentions of the central bank to hit a given inflation target. The nature and extent of commitments dominated, as so-called open mouth operations became an additional way to influence monetary conditions with Bank Rate pegged at ground zero. The huge interest in examining the words of central bankers was certainly empowering if not exactly elucidating.

The NK argument that monetary policy can only work through the management of expectations is not a universal result as it relies, unsurprisingly, on particular assumptions.

In these models, financial markets are complete in which a representative agent can spring into life and financial wealth is allocated over an infinite life. Idiosyncratic risk in these economies can be hedged and asset prices depend on state-contingent payoffs. In this case, the price of financial assets are not influenced by changes in their net supply, as demand is perfectly elastic. But, on careful reflection, it seems quite possible though that demand curves for assets, particularly those which are issued in large quantities, may become downward sloping, in which case changes in net supply can affect their relative prices. This possibility then means that the relative supply of money or credit can influence market interest rates and impact directly on expenditure paths without having to rely on pure signalling effects. It is this possibility which gives quantitative easing its influence, particularly in abnormal times. We will return to the question of normal and abnormal times, and indeed one enduring parable about central banking is that it is about crisis management.

6.2.2   Effectiveness

Early work on the impact of large-scale asset purchases as a tool of monetary policy probably began following 'Operation Twist' in the United States in 1961. Although not full quantitative easing in the sense of being financed by base money creation, this operation involved Federal Reserve purchases of long-term bonds (financed by sales of short-term Treasury bills) as well as a change in Treasury issuance with the aim of lowering long-term interest rates. Franco Modigliani and Richard Sutch (1966) found that this operation had no significant effect on bond yields, though more recent work by Eric Swanson (2011) has found that this operation had some significant market impact. In one of those interesting bits of interpretation the studies, separated by over forty years, agreed on the basic impact in terms of basis points on yields but not on the significance of the operation: 10–20bp was not considered a large number in the 1960s but seems to be thought to be significant today.

More recently, the QE programme implemented by the Bank of Japan from 2001 to 2006 generated new interest in unconventional monetary policy implemented through large-scale asset purchases. In a survey of empirical evidence in the Japanese case, Hiroshi Ugai

(2007) found mixed evidence. He concluded that the evidence suggested that QE had some signalling impact on market expectations in the sense of confirming that interest rates would remain low for some time, but the evidence on whether the QE operations had any direct effect on bond yields or risk premia was mixed. However, Ben Bernanke, Vince Reinhart and Brian Sack (2004), examining the Japanese experience with QE, found little by way of announcement effects but some evidence from a macro-finance yield curve to suggest that Japanese yields were roughly 50bp lower than expected during QE. Unsurprisingly perhaps, the QE programmes implemented in the aftermath of the 2008 financial crisis have led to a dramatic increase in research on this topic. Most notably, the Federal Reserve's QE programme spawned a large and rapidly growing literature.

In the US case, despite a wide range of methodological approaches, there is near-unanimous agreement that the US programme had significant effects on longer-term bond yields, though estimates of the scale of the effect vary considerably; for example, a survey by the Federal Bank of New York (Joe Gagnon et al., 2010) found that the $300bn of US bond purchases, which amount to approximately 2 per cent of GDP, resulted in drops of some 90bp in US ten-year Treasuries, while Arvind Krisnamurthy and Anette Vissing-Jorgensen (2010) find that a reduction in public debt outstanding of around 20 per cent of GDP would reduce yields by something like 60–115 basis points. So far, the United Kingdom's QE programme has attracted less interest. Empirical estimates of the impact of the initial £125bn of QE and then the full £200bn (14 per cent of GDP) on UK gilt yields by André Meier (2009) and then a Bank of England study by Mike Joyce and colleagues (2010) suggest that yields are some 40–100 bp lower than they would have been in the absence of QE. My own students, for example, see Evren Caglar et al. (2011) did, however, suggest that the event study methodology may have overestimated the effects because of the dominant, possibly exaggerated, impact of the first rather than the subsequent six announcements. These studies, mostly conducted by central banks themselves, have to confront at least three issues as far as financial prices are concerned. What is the initial impact? What is the ongoing or more permanent impact? How do financial market participants now expect the central bank to react to news in terms of expected QE and further asset purchases? If the latter predicts the first, then the impact will look increasingly limited.

Even if a significant impact can be demonstrated on market interest rates along the term structure, the more important question is whether the economy has been better stabilised than it might have been in the absence of QE. Such a counterfactual is rather hard to run, but it is the bread and butter of economics. Consider an economy that is suffering a financial shock or a pandemic-related shutdown such that borrowing and lending activities, as well as overall activity and exchange, are constrained. This prevents the circulation of capital to new technologies and leads to the increasing prevalence of older technologies and will tend to hamper the accrual of technological change. If we add in a rebalancing of private portfolios, so that households and firms plan to run down financial indebtedness, which is another way of saying that they start to save, and we add in a multiplier-type story that means lower incomes lead to more savings and a channel of magnification, by which all trade competitors also undergo the same process, we can start to understand both the rapidity and depth of the recession. Much of this response to the financial crisis was thus to do with actual economic capacity, which would fall as the fraction of less productive firms increased, and a change in the perceived 'safe' level of debt in the economy would result in a persistent downward response in activity, and all monetary policy could do in these circumstances was to offer something of a softer landing than would otherwise have been the case. It ought not to have produced immediate strong growth but simply curtailed the length of the recession, which it did.

Once we move away from separating the monetary from the financial and directly influencing prices and quantities in the loanable funds market, monetary policy stops being a technical matter of repair but can shift the economic structure itself and hence find itself more

The transmission mechanism of monetary policy

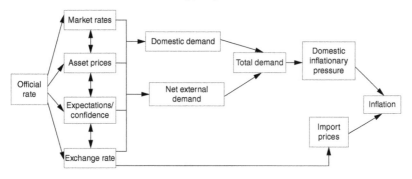

FIGURE 6.4 The MPC 1999 view of the MTM

obviously propelled into the political arena of distribution and prosperity itself. Indeed, in the very long run, Fernand Braudel (1979)
points to the movement of economic and financial power from
Amsterdam to London and then New York as a way of confirming a
link between society, economy and finance. The technical matter of
monetary exchange masks and forces economic and social change and
yet in our own real time we are mostly oblivious to it.

As far as theory, there is also a bigger picture being drawn. If
even reasonably safe assets like government bonds had risk premia
that might be alleviated by changes in their net supply, it implies that
the demand curves for these assets are inelastic. If demand is inelastic
for government bonds at a given price they are likely to be inelastic for
other more risky assets. Changes in risk premia can then be thought
of as part of the monetary transmission mechanism as they lie within
the (at last partial) control of the policymaker. We quickly learnt that
the standard or basic picture of a simple monetary transmission
mechanism – Figure 6.4 shows the MPC diagram from 1999 – was
more than a little out of date as it did not explicitly consider risk
premia, banks or money supply, and all policy was simply directed
through the official interest rate. What we had was a model of the
impact of policy that was concentrated on controlling domestic
demand through traditional channels alone.

6.3   INCORPORATING RISKY BORROWING AND LENDING

We are about to move away decisively from the model in which the macroeconomy corresponds closely to that of a single household, with income, expenditure and output all determined by the choices of this one representative agent, which has been the basic building block for much policy thought. However, I shall examine what happens when we unbundle the economy into a saver household and a borrower household who each face different interest rates.[4] We can also easily call these households asset rich and debt poor, but let us keep with savers and borrowers for the moment; then we can examine the equilibrium from an unconstrained and supply constrained perspective and consider the case for macro-prudential instruments (MPIs) as a Pigovian tax, one which aims to ensure that the private costs of supply credit do not diverge from the costs likely to be borne by society.

In the type of model where there is more than one interest rate, policy may operate either through the standard short rate set by the central bank or through the interest rates available in the bond market. When we consider the standard consumer problem, for a saver, consumption growth is proportional to the deposit (or bond) rate available to savers so that when interest rates go up, consumption is delayed today and put back until tomorrow, and this means that expected consumption growth is positive. Thus, the current level of consumption by savers is a negative function of both the deposit or bond rate, and so the pool of savings is increasing in these interest rates.

If we go on to consider the same problem from the perspective of a borrower-household rather than a saver-household, the consumption of borrowers is tilted by the rate of interest they have to pay on their borrowing, which is the basic policy (or deposit) rate plus a premium related to the costs of obtaining funds from a financial intermediary and is normally called an external finance premium.

---

[4] This section draws on my work with Luisa Corrado, Germana Corrado and Ivan Buratta.

This premium might be related to the costs of monitoring and screening the ability of a firm to pay back loans but also about the risk of that lending which will have an economy-wide and specific component related to firm-level risk. The quantity of borrowing available from a financial intermediary is capped by some link to the present value of collateral and further constrained by any limits imposed on the amount that can be lent, relative to borrower-household income. Accordingly, the growth in net lending cannot typically be greater than the growth in the value of collateral offered so that any policy that acts on the borrowing constraint directly will act to reduce net lending; we shall return to this point. The key thing here is that borrower-households are sensitive to changes in lending rates rather than savings rates.

Although households ultimately provide the funds for borrowers, these savings are channelled through a financial intermediary, typically a bank, which will wish to maximise profits by lending at a rate that is a mark-up over the costs of providing funding, the substantive part of which is the interest paid on deposits. In the absence of risk premia or, in a perfectly competitive world of loans supply, the marginal price of a loan will equal the marginal costs of funding, and loan rate will equal the deposit rate. Ideally, the marginal cost of finance would then equal the marginal return to society from that unit of capital. But normally the financial intermediary supplies funds in a costly manner because borrowers need to be screened and monitored. The financial premium places a wedge between the two. And if the supply of funds through financial intermediation does not price social welfare, we may very easily have more (or less) lending than is socially optimal. Of course, more would imply a boom and less would lead to a slump. This channel can not only amplify unwarranted fluctuations, but it can also trigger them.

There are a number of possible reasons why intermediation may not price social welfare accurately and may lead to distortions in asset prices. First, the borrower may walk away from the debt related to an asset purchase and choose not to pay the principal back and leave the

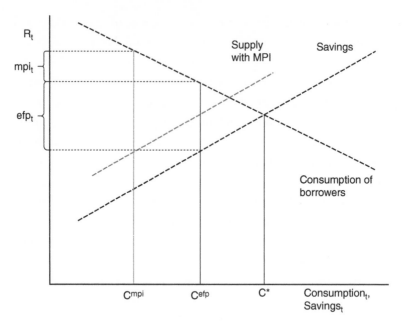

FIGURE 6.5 The external finance premium and MPIs

bank holding the loss rather than borrower. In this case, the value of the asset to the borrower will be distorted upwards because he will not pay any losses. A similar phenomenon may be found in the banks themselves, which may feel that they need not make provisions for losses if the state (via taxes on savers) will pay, and in this there will be more lending than when the costs of losses are internal rather than external to the bank. Finally, if asset values underpin lending, household consumption may, in the borrower household, or even in aggregate very strongly with asset prices and become somewhat too volatile. Ultimately any failure or extended 'stop' in the financial intermediary function will prevent the ability of households to borrow or lend in the presence of temporary shocks in their income and share their risks with other households.

Figure 6.5 illustrates the basic case for some controls on lending in the form of so-called MPIs, that flows from our analysis. The supply of savings, consumption forgone by saver-households, increases in the real interest rate, $[R_t]$, which we can think of as some combination of the deposit rate and the bond rate. The level of aggregate consumption is set by the $[R_t]$, which determines the level of consumption. At the unconstrained equilibrium, the external finance premium, the wedge between borrower and saver interest rates, is driven to zero and consumption is maximised at $[C^*]$ for borrowers. When we add in an external finance premium, the level of consumption for borrowers is lower and there is less call on the pool of savings. Indeed, to as we move to the left of $[C^*]$, the consumption of borrowers falls and that of savers increases, and implies that the consumption of these two types of households may move in opposite directions and may be negatively correlated. The composition of demand in this economy is determined by the real interest rate $[R_t]$, as it determines the split between borrower and saver consumption. The market-determined external finance premium, $[efp_t]$, reflects the sensitivity of borrower household consumption and I show one possible equilibrium $[C^{efp}]$, where consumption by borrower households is constrained. Note that the external finance premium falls when real rates rise and increases when it falls.[5] In other words, when the economy is growing rapidly, in what economists call an expansion, and the deposit and bond rates, which are closely tied to the policy rate, tend to rise, lending conditions may actually relax, and when the economy is in a rut with low policy rates, lending conditions may well be quite restrictive.

In a general equilibrium, we may expect something like the mechanism to hold because high policy rates, low lending spreads and an economic expansion (and vice versa) all go hand in hand as part of the economic narrative. However, if the supply of savings, which is intermediated through banks, does not price the social costs of lending, by which we mean the costs to both sets of households

---

[5] Note also that changes in the lending constraint will change the size of the external finance premium.

from an excessively volatile business cycle in which jobs may be lost or future taxes that will be levied to provide support for broken financial intermediaries, then it makes sense to consider mechanisms that limit supply of lending in a manner that is not simply regulated by policy rates. It may thus be appropriate to place a 'tax' on supply and this will tend to reduce further the consumption of borrowers. The tax can be any policy that reduces the supply of savings at every given interest rate and may include actual taxes on financial transactions, as proposed by Tobin, or simply policies that limit supply by requiring banks to show more circumspection in lending, the basic result of which is to further limit the consumption of borrower-households to the point $[C^{mpi}]$ at which the existing magnitude of external finance premium is augmented. The lower level of consumption here by borrowers is designed to reduce the build-up in financial risks over the business cycle and can be modified in a manner separate from the policy rate and offer policymakers an extra degree of freedom. Such policies may not be wholly popular, as David Ricardo (1819, pp. 48–49) suggests:

> In all rich countries there is a number of men forming what is called the moneyed class: these men are engaged in no trade, but live on the interest of their money, which is employed in discounting bills, or in loans to the more industrious part of the community. The bankers too employ a large capital on the same objects. The capital so employed forms a circulating capital of a large amount, and is employed, in larger or small proportions, by all the different trades of a country.

But are designed to reduce the violence of economic fluctuations by dampening their acceleration by financial intermediation.

6.4 MACRO-PRUDENTIAL INSTRUMENTS

There is no established workhorse model (yet) for understanding financial frictions in the economy and there are a number of models vying for professional central adoption. But Simon Hall (2009) provides a useful taxonomy. In a manner similar to the analysis in the previous section, he reminds us that an increase in any financial friction will tend to increase the interest rate wedge between those who provide capital and the cost of capital paid by firms or households; such a wedge will tend to depress output and employment. The story is similar to the analysis of the inefficiency of taxation of an intermediate product, with capital playing the role of an intermediate product. The argument here is that taxing an intermediate good distorts the allocation of factors of production between intermediate and final, or consumption, goods and so leads to a smaller overall level of income in the economy.

The legs of the argument are that an increase in financial frictions acts to increase the price of capital, reduce its deployment and increase both the ratio of output to capital ratio and to consumption accordingly, in what is called capital shallowing. Through the standard Cobb-Douglas production function – which states that output is a function of two factors capital and labour, as well as their productivity – the labour-capital ratio rises along with the fall in the capital-output ratio. The lower level of capital eventually induces a longer run fall in output. The argument goes through in the opposite direction with a fall in the size of financial frictions. Indeed, under this kind of analysis financial frictions are embedded in the supply side of the economy and may be particularly hard to understand in an NK model, which concentrates on demand and cost-push shocks in the production of goods. When we take financial frictions seriously, it turns out that reductions in these frictions will tend to induce changes in output and inflation that look very much like increases in potential supply and will tend to be accommodated by monetary policymakers. MPIs are thus any attempt to offset changes in the frictions by offsetting changes in taxes so that a booming economy experiencing a lessening in frictions may be subject to an increase in its MPI tax, and an economy in recession and increasing financial frictions may be treated to a fall in the tax in order to attenuate the impact on output.

6.4.1   Monetary and Financial Stability

It is entirely possible to take the view that financial and monetary policy should simply run in tandem so that managing the latter well also requires attention to be paid and information to be exchanged in the pursuit of the two objectives jointly. Indeed the historical record suggests a similar juxtaposition – that the nature and scope of the regulation of financial intermediation was closely linked to the monetary policy regime and the immediate post-war period with the Bretton Woods system of fixed-but-adjustable exchange rates was associated with both extensive regulation of the financial system and also the virtual elimination of banking crises, apart from Brazil in 1962.[6]

The cost of such extensive supervision was such that it is probably the case that the financial system did not allocate investment particularly efficiently over this period and momentum for deregulation built up to a considerable degree. In principle therefore, there is a trade-off between designing instruments to stabilise the financial system and preventing excessively volatile financial outcomes and ensuring that the financial sector retains the correct incentives to locate investment opportunities and allocate funds accordingly. It is not initially clear that deployment of macroprudential instruments (MPIs) in a single currency area covered by one central bank can work independently of further controls on the movement of capital across other currency regions, particularly when financial intermediaries have interests overseas. So what we are looking for are instruments that will work given some form of monetary policy regime that closely resembles what we currently have in place here. This implies some overriding equivalence in financial rules.

From the perspective of monetary policymakers, the initial debate, as explained in the previous chapters, was whether inflation

---

[6] See Franklin Allen and Douglas Gale, Chapter 1, on this observation.

targeting could be modified so that an additional instrument could be used to stabilise financial imbalances or directly control the extent of financial intermediation. The answer that emerged prior to the full force of the financial crisis that was felt, was that there was limited scope to do much. As previously outlined, Charlie Bean (2004) argues that it is optimal under discretion to ignore any asset price boom and only mitigate any fallout on collapse; under commitment it turns out there is even less incentive to stabilise output when the economy is overheating. Lars Svensson (2009) considers that 'flexible inflation targeting' that stabilises output and inflation may have an occasionally binding constraint to ensure financial stability and booms (busts) can justify an inflation undershoot (overshoot), as well as an extended period of adjustment back to target. Even if a limited number of modifications to monetary policy operating procedures are sufficient to stabilise macroeconomic outcomes, they may not be enough to realise financial stability for which appropriate supervision and regulation, perhaps at a granular and systematic level, are unlikely to be replaced simply by new instruments.

Actually, it turned out that another instrument was developed, but this was quantitative easing and was designed to deal directly with the lower zero bound constraint. As explained in this chapter, the purchase of gilts under QE seems to have driven medium-term yields down by the extent to which they might have been expected to fall, had short-term interest rates been lowered by some 2–4 per cent. The swap of reserves for bonds did not palpably augment bank lending, but the counterfactual – with a changing regulatory framework for liquidity in prospect and a large shortfall in output below its pre-2007 trend – is rather hard to evaluate. There seems to be no attempt to consider using this stock of bonds held to help regulate the financial system on an ongoing basis. When financial markets are sensitive to risk, financial intermediaries cannot create sufficient liquidity and so in principle the central bank can regulate the flow of liquidity over the business cycle in order to prevent excessive amplification of the business cycle by financial intermediaries.[7]

In fact, a number of non-conventional monetary policy tools have been developed here and overseas that might have implications for both monetary and financial stability. Some recent work found that each of a number of non-conventional tools augmented the stabilising properties of the interest rate rule from the asset side of commercial bank balance sheets (via reserves) and the liability side (via bank capital) of the same balance sheet, as well as helping to meet the preferences of households to hold short-run liquid assets, and so implied a possible reduction in financial volatility. Overall, non-conventional tools would seem to have some financial stability considerations, there is (i) guidance or signalling, which includes the recent fashion for central bank forecasts of policy rates for extended periods, which fits in with both the New Keynesian orthodoxy, in which monetary operations do not impact on net wealth and therefore do not affect consumption but might impact on the expected path of interest rates, also with an older tradition of the 'Governor's eyebrows'; (ii) there have been temporary liquidity injections of reserve money, or extended OMOs, which are essentially QE; (iii) the direct purchase of distressed assets and on the fiscal side, there is bank recapitalisation and credit easing and although in the latter case this has come to mean the composition of the central bank balance sheet in the United States, rather than direct lending to the private sector. So I think we have (i) signalling; (ii) liquidity; (iii) asset support; and (iv) fiscal policy. Clearly, there are elements of one in each of the others and any operation is surely tantamount to a signal of some sort, as well as providing some fiscal support by reducing the cost of debt service. Indeed one might argue that each of these can be viewed through the lens of MPI.

---

[7] See Douglas Gale (2011) on this point, who also argues that when risk appetite is high, too much liquidity can be created.

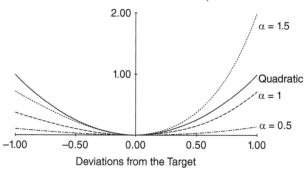

LINEX and Quadratic Losses Compared

FIGURE 6.6 Asymmetric losses

6.4.2 *How to Value Misses: The Loss Function*

MPIs might involve a large number of possible instruments including capital, margin, liquidity and equity-loan ratios. There is a danger that, given the recent experience of an overextended financial system, the mindset for the pursuit of MPIs implies an asymmetric concern with the stability of the financial system, rather like that with the foundation of a building or the construction of a dam, so that we are in general concerned with reining in excessive intermediation rather than increasing overall activity. Put rather bluntly: who on the FPC would lose their job if the financial system were considered to be excessively safe compared to the converse?[8]

An asymmetric loss function does not necessarily have to be pursued asymmetrically. The policymaker simply has to pursue a slightly different target. This is because minimising the expected loss of an asymmetric loss function, such as that presented in Figure 6.6, is not achieved by targeting the minimum at zero but at some point in the opposite direction of the steeper asymmetric loss. As drawn, expected losses would be minimised to the left of zero, whereas for a symmetric loss function, zero would do it. In fact it would be given by

---

[8] The Financial Policy Committee (FPC) of the Bank of England is charged with thinking about and implementing MPIs.

a term in governing the asymmetry of the function and the likely size of any shocks. So the target will be driven further to the left for larger shocks and greater asymmetry in the loss function. Once this principle has been established it makes sense to develop steady-state targets that build in a precautionary target for more liquidity, capital and equity to loan ratios than a strict minimum might imply. Both David Miles and John Vickers have made this case publicly.

6.4.3   Target and Instruments

As has been explored in this book, we want to count the number of independent instruments and objectives. In the current set-up, the MPC will continue to set Bank Rate to pursue the inflation target and it will be the FPC that will have instruments at its disposal to pursue financial stability. To the extent that we cannot be sure about the impact of any instrument, Brainard uncertainty introduces a trade-off between the achievement of the target and the minimisation of uncertainty induced by the use of an instrument. There are two further problems here in the case of MPIs: (i) there is likely to be considerably more uncertainty with a set of untried instruments that may also have a correlation structure with each other, but (ii) also because they may alter the behaviour of the financial system, they will directly affect the impact of any given stance of monetary policy on the real economy.

On the first point, it might be that we can treat MPIs as a portfolio of instruments that jointly will reduce the idiosyncratic risk of using any one new instrument. But without specification, calibration or testing of the impact of any one instrument in combination with the others, we cannot probably be very sure at all whether such a portfolio of instruments will be available. Ideally we want to think about which instruments may be used but how they might be used together and in a manner that does not induce greater uncertainty into the operation of monetary policy. Figure 6.7 shows how the use of MPIs may improve the trade-off in uncertainty-space available to policymakers, so that rather than the line ABC, the policymaker will

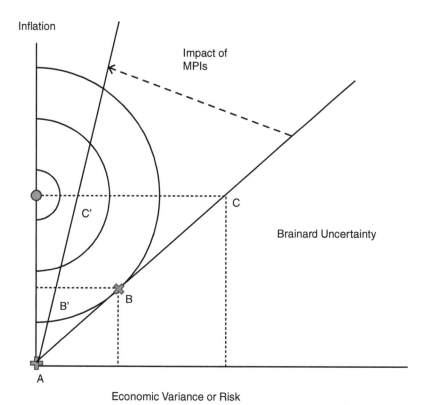

FIGURE 6.7 MPIs and the policy trade-off

be able to choose along [ABC] and would prefer a point fairly near to [C'], where inflation is at target and an undershoot is no longer preferred.

To the extent that changing the constraints faced by financial intermediaries will alter the financial conditions, as the choice made on the quantity and price of intermediation will be affected, there may not only be an impact on the appropriate stance of monetary policy but also an impact on the appropriate MPIs conditioned on the monetary policy stance.

Consider a world in which the monetary policymaker wishes to smooth the response of consumption to a large negative shock to aggregate demand and reduces interest rates faced by collateral-constrained consumers. This is the situation we find ourselves in as we enter the third decade of the twenty-first century. Simultaneously, financial stability may be considered to be threatened and various MPIs may be tightened, which would act against the interest rate changes made by the monetary policymaker and may need further or extended lower rates of interest rates. If, on the other hand, sufficient precautionary moves had been made by the FPC in advance there may be no immediate conflict.

6.4.4 Operating MPIs

In principle, MPIs may be used to help stabilise the financial system over the business cycle. There are, though, quite separate issues to consider when designing MPIs to help stabilise a reasonably well-functioning financial system, which might be thought of as leaning against the wind, and the correct responses for a highly vulnerable and under-capitalised financial system. The former implies the use of cyclical instruments to prevent a problematic build-up of risk and the latter some attention to the superstructure of the financial system with individual firms and the sector as a whole not only able to withstand shocks but sufficiently robust as not to amplify them.

And yet the financial system is already undergoing a considerable deleveraging that has involved a build-up in core capital, increased holdings of liquid assets and greater margin requirements. In a sense the financial system is moving from a loose regime to another tighter one, but too fast a transition may have unwanted macroeconomic consequences.

The extent to which difficulties in obtaining finance may constrain the investment or consumption plans of some firms and households may imply that although what may be optimal are tougher long-run regulatory targets, there may be some sense in thinking about how to allow the divergence from these targets for extended periods (rather like a credible fiscal regime that ensures sustainable public finances is one more likely to allow the full force of automatic stabilisers to operate). In this sense, if banks are forced to observe a target at all times, this may be counterproductive for the system as a whole. It is an example of Goodhart's (2008) taxi where the last remaining taxi at a railway station at night could not accept a fare because of a regulation that at least one taxi had to be at the railway station all the time.

One of the results to emerge from the analysis of monetary policy is that the control of a forward-looking system is best achieved by setting predictable policy that allows forward-looking agents to plan conditional on the likely policy response. There has been considerable work to suggest that the impact of monetary policy is a function of both the level and the path of interest rates, which is likely to be closely related to predictability. As well as evaluating instruments, any FPC will have to pay careful attention to how expectations of changes in MPIs are formed and whether partial adjustment towards some intermediate or cyclical target for a given level of capital, liquidity or loan-to-value will be adopted. The alternative of jumping to new requirements may induce large adjustment costs for the financial sector and the use of considerable resources to predict future movements in requirements. The private sector may also be induced to bring forward or delay financial transactions depending on the expectations of collateral requirements. In a slightly different context, the pre-announced abolition of double rates of mortgage interest relief at source (MIRAS) may have played a role in stoking some aspects of the house price boom of the late 1980s as it brought forward house price purchases, similar to the impact of the temporary Stamp Duty holiday during the COVID-19 crisis.[9] Under some circumstances, such a response reflecting strong intertemporal switching may be entirely what a macro-prudential framework may wish to bring about but, more generally, when agents are well informed and forward-looking, some thought has to be given to developing a framework for understanding agents' responses to any expected or pre-announced changes in the rules governing financial intermediation.

[9] See Nigel Lawson (1992) on this point.

6.4.5 Monetary Policy and Liquidity

The nexus of MPIs and monetary policy does suggest that there may be a complementarity.[10] The widespread adoption of non-conventional monetary policies has provided some evidence of the efficacy of liquidity and asset purchases for offsetting the lower zero bound. Central banks have thus been reminded as to the effectiveness of extended open market operations as a supplementary tool of monetary policy. These tools can essentially be thought of as fiscal instruments, as they issue interest rate–bearing central bank liabilities. These instruments are placed in the government's present value budget constraint and the consequences of these operations can be understood within the context of a macroeconomic model of banking and money. The responses of the Federal Reserve balance sheet to the financial crisis can be mimicked. Specifically, the role of central bank reserves swaps for bond and capital and also the impact of changing the composition of the central bank balance sheet can be examined. It is found that such policies can significantly enhance the ability of the central bank to stabilise the economy. This is because balance sheet operations supply (remove) liquidity to a financial market that is otherwise short (long) of liquidity and hence allows other financial spreads to move less violently over the cycle to compensate. As already outlined, these liquidity operations act like negative taxes on financial intermediation.

The case for the systematic use of balance sheet or reserve or bank capital policies can also be examined. Compared to a model that does not explicitly model bank balance sheets, recent models can deliver an endogenous dynamic response for various risk premia and for the supply of loans and deposits. It is possible by using standard methods, to compare the responses of an artificial economy with and without reserve injections. Having approximated the welfare of the representative household, it can be found that the economy in which

---

[10] See my work with Luisa Corrado, Jack Meaning and Tobias Schuler in which we look at these complementarities.

commercial banks have an endogenous choice over reserve holdings performs better in welfare terms than when commercial banks do not have such a choice. The holding of reserves or capital over the business cycle acts as a substitute for more costly provision of illiquid commercial bank assets and thus reduces the volatility of interest spreads to shocks, and varying the availability of reserves over expansions and contractions, acts to help stabilise the impulse from the monetary sector. The parables are interesting, as are the lags. First the policy. Then the economy responds. And then the models examine plausibility and counterfactuals. Judgement is conditioned on experience and it informs theoretical progress.

However, the work, in my view, is rather at an early stage and has yet to be tested under more uncertainty over instrument choice and its effectiveness. It would be useful to summarise some of the emergent literature as well; there are a number of missing elements to the analysis: (i) the consideration of fiscal policy, which if excessively expansionary may induce increases in liquidity premia, or may be in a position to offset liquidity shortages by trading long-run debt for short run liabilities; and (ii) the consideration of non-linearities or discontinuities in responses, for example, from bankruptcy. That said, there may be some gains from jointly determined MPIs and standard interest rate responses, conditioned on sustainable public finances, which may lead to welfare gains for households.

Following the financial crisis, and the need to undo the Separation Principle for monetary and financial stability, we can agree that there are missing instruments and there is a hunt to locate ones that can be employed, or suggested for us, by the FPC. I remain concerned as to how long-run targets for capital, liquidity and asset-mix and lending criteria will be set, and whether a bias to over-regulation may be set in motion. It is not at all clear how many new cyclical MPIs will interact with each other and impact on the setting of monetary policy. A reverse causation is also possible, whereby the stance of monetary policy may have implications for the correct setting of MPIs. The management of expectations over any

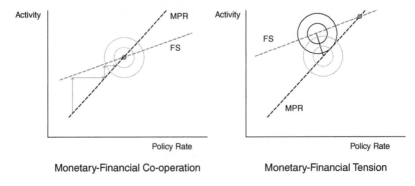

FIGURE 6.8 Monetary and financial co-operation

announcements of changing MPIs will be a crucial area in a modern financial system – it was probably significantly easier in a world of extensive capital and exchange controls that characterised the immediate post-war period. All that said, early results from a new generation of macro models do suggest that there may be significant gains from getting the calibration of these new instruments right, but much work remains to be done.

6.5 THE INTERACTION OF GOVERNMENT DEBT, MONETARY POLICY AND FINANCIAL POLICY

In some senses the classical monetary model places a lot of the action off stage and so brings into focus the heroic role of the monetary policymaker, who hopes to avoid Athenian tragedy. Actually, there are at least two key interactions that both limit and channel the actions of the monetary policymaker: fiscal policy and the operations of the financial sector. A further interaction concerns that between the financial sector and the fiscal policymaker, as we consider the role that public sector purchases of financial institutions played in stabilising the financial sector and also the extent to which financial sector liabilities are hedged with government IOUs of one sort or another. We must have a happy triumvirate.

The fiscal policymaker is typically charged with respecting the government's present value budget constraint, which means establishing plans for expenditure and taxes that mean the level of debt is expected to be (low and) stable in normal states of nature, which typically mean extended peacetime or economic expansions. The financial sector operates to translate savings into stable returns by intermediating between current investors and consumers and future investors and consumers, otherwise known as savers. The stable income streams offered by the government sector may be of value to the private sector as it seeks nominal or real payments that are stable in the face of business cycle shocks, and may provide a benchmark for the construction of other market interest rates. The monetary policymaker sets the costs of funding for the financial sector and also has a huge influence on the costs of funding government debt. The level of economic activity depends to a large degree on the financial and fiscal sector, so it is an outcome of the central bank's responses to the behaviour of these two sectors.

I am not necessarily arguing that there is a need for explicit co-ordination. But the William Nordhaus (1994) example of monetary-fiscal interactions may be instructive if not completely comparable to that of the financial sector and our triumvirate. Consider a y-axis representing economic activity and the x-axis, policy rate." Also accept that a conservative bank chooses a preferred level of interest rates [MPR] for every level of activity on a path that will tend to drive the economy to its preferred point. The financial sector (FS, let us put the fiscal sector aside for the moment), may be stabilising and act to drive up activity when it is below the socially preferred point and help bear down on it when activity is above the socially preferred point. This is because asset prices and market interest rates may act to generate levels of activity that act as a conduit from monetary policy to the overall level of activity, back to some notion of long-run equilibrium.

So in normal times, the central bank relies on the financial sector to be stabilising and carry out a large part of the stabilising response. But in times of boom and bust it may stoke up excessive fluctuations in activity, which begs the question of why any financial agent pursues plans that differ from those the central bank might choose? One, because it has different preferences; two, because it has different information; and three, because it will not bear the consequences of its choices. As a result, without any co-ordination, the Nash equilibrium may imply high interest rates, but the respective Bliss Points for monetary policy, MPR, and for the financial sector, FS, imply a contract curve along which losses for each policymaker will be less than under the Nash equilibrium, which means that some form of co-operation is to be preferred. Whether that co-operation can be constructed in a manner that brings us firmly back to our preferred equilibrium is the key question for the economic settlement after the crisis.

6.6   CONCLUDING REMARKS

I am not sure that wisdom and foresight has necessarily been lost in the search for a simple, credible monetary policy by the money minders. The ultimate decisions of any policy rely on judgement and that can, unfortunately, remain faulty even in the presence of that self-same wisdom and foresight while both judgement and intuition are often formed with reference to the experience of working with models. However, because no model can provide a perfect guide to the menu of choices, we must learn not only to choose which ones are useful for policymakers but also think through the implications of our models being wrong. The robustification of policy may mean working through the implications, however unpalatable, of the unlikely as well as the preferred circumstances.

Some difficult lessons were learnt over the financial crisis and were rehearsed again in 2020 and bear repeating. First and rather obviously, inflation targeting alone cannot prevent boom and bust and needs to be augmented with more instruments and better judgement. The operations of the financial sector through the creation of various elements of broad money and also at the lower zero bound, as it changes its demand for central bank money, complicates choices about the path and long run level of Bank Rate. Policy rates are not being ever so slightly perturbed near their long-run normal level, but the duration of rates at very low levels is stretching patience. MPC members did not take on the job to set interest rates in order never to move them over the duration of their appointments.

Not only do financial frictions complicate the choices of policy-makers because changes in the financial settlement may make the transmission of policy hard to gauge, but they have always acted through both the traditional supply and demand side. This means that such frictions make judgements about capacity even harder. Recall that the key monetary policy judgement typically involves working out the current and likely future levels of spare capacity in the economy. The sensible application of liquidity and capital targets via macro-prudential policy may seem likely to reduce business cycle variance albeit at some cost of permanent output, and so transitional judgements will have to be even more careful than usual not to treat the permanent as the temporary and vice versa.

The interactions between fiscal, financial and monetary policy not withstanding, we also now accept that fiscal policy as well as underpinning aggregate demand can also provide support to fragile financial institutions, if and only if the private sector wishes to hold government IOUs. This further contingent role for government debt makes the case for slightly more conservative fiscal policy than aggregate demand considerations would themselves imply. During the long and lonely march back to normality, public debt as a fraction of output will take, at best, a generation to return to 'normal' and as long as demand remains inelastic, positive or negative changes in net supply will impact on price and complicate choices on Bank Rate. It would seem that plotting the policy path will be considerably more complicated during recovery and normality and thus requires even more public explanation than we have had in the past by the money minders. And the urgency is heightened so as to ensure that the democratic mandate for price and financial stability is not threatened by the lack of attention being paid to institutional strategies for co-ordination with the fiscal policies of H. M. Treasury and the powerful role of financial interests. I leave the (nearly) final word to economist and banker, Henry Thornton (1802):

> Paper Credit has, on this account, been highly important to us. Our former familiarity with it prepared us for more extended use of it. And our experience of its power of supplying the want of gold in time of difficulty and peril, is a circumstance which, though it ought not to encourage a general disuse of count, may justly add to the future confidence of the nation.

Epilogues

These two epilogues present practical applications of money minder thinking to two major policy problems that faced the UK and the world in 2016 and then in 2020. The long march to increased globalisation that would lead to "increased shares for all" from trade juddered to a halt following the financial crisis and, given sluggish economic growth subsequently, opened up a debate about the true costs of economic openness, particular to labour flows. This manifested itself in the UK as a push for referendum on continued membership of the EU. Much of the debate in the run up to the referendum and subsequently once the people had spoken was on the likely, or forecasted, economic effects of a decision to leave. The debate then rapidly descended into a search for clues as to whether the fears or gains from leaving had been exaggerated by popular forecasting narratives. And indeed whether we should rely on the views of 'experts'. The first epilogue, written in early 2017, thus confronts the value of economic forecasting against the sharp focus of a country trying to understand to what it had just agreed. The money minder needs to tell a number of stories that are consistent within their own terms, that is the purpose of a model. But as she cannot really know which story will unfold, she, as a consequence of outlining these stories, also has to be prepared to respond to any of the outcomes. And so this is the message of the second epilogue, written in the spring of 2020 just as the magnitude of the COVID-19 pandemic was becoming clearer. Here I make the money minder case for supporting fiscal policy by helping to create fiscal space with lower funding costs and absorbing any excess issuance of public debt. This was a "once-in-a-century" shock and outside the distributions beloved by econometricians and yet precisely the time that monetary policy – if credibly committed to price stability – could provide support to the functioning of markets and provide support for an economy in temporary free-fall. But with a clear eye on how to do so without undermining long price and monetary stability. For which the eye may need the support of a commitment to exit from extraordinary measures when we recovered. The absence of that clear commitment will test credibility increasingly as the recovery builds momentum and price pressures build. The critical ability to act flexibly if hemmed in by hard won credibility and can disappear with it, depressingly easily.

Epilogue 1: Why Forecast?*

> The role of prediction in economics involves a fundamental tension. On the one hand, much of the economics is concerned with prediction. On the other, economic predictions are notoriously unreliable. It is, in fact, tempting to see the economist as the trapeze-performer who tends to miss the cross-bar, or as the jockey who keeps falling off his horse ... However, it cannot be doubted that prediction is one of the central pre-occupations of economics. Policy prescriptions will inter alia involve relating alternative courses of actions to predicted outcomes. Even the description of observed trends of unemployment, poverty, living standards, etc., would tend to lead one to ask questions about the future. Not all of economics is concerned with predicting, but the central role of prediction in economics can scarcely be denied.
>
> A. K. Sen, *Prediction and Economic Theory*, 1986

There has been an intense debate about the rationale behind economic prediction or forecasting, triggered by a sequence of forecast errors before and after the financial crisis and more recently by a 'surprisingly' buoyant economy after the 2016 referendum on the United Kingdom's membership in the European Union. Some economists argue that the value of a forecast is strictly related to its forecast accuracy. Others argue that what matters is less the forecast errors but the stories that are revealed by such errors. The former might be thought to relate the value of economic forecasting solely in terms of a statistical criterion and the latter to the need to concentrate on structural relationships between economic variables that will be subject to errors (or shocks) but which can be treated as stable. I argue that the forecast process is inherently subject to large errors, and so is a hazardous exercise, but that does not by itself invalidate the exercise because both the producers and consumers of forecasts understand that errors will occur. This knowledge throws up a clear obligation for

* A version of this essay appeared in the National Institute Economic Review, "Why Forecast?, 2017;239(1):F4–F9.

producers to explain errors before the fact by use of uncertainty or scenario plots and for consumers to treat the forecasts with caution.

EI.I   A MUG'S GAME

Economic forecasters ought to be thankful for pollsters, otherwise they might look very bad indeed. The story that has frequently been repeated is that a recession was forecast in the event of a vote to leave the European Union and because there had been no recession, economic forecasters had let us down. This story is not quite right, for example, in May 2016 the *National Institute Economic Review* simply argued that growth would be broadly unaffected in 2016 by a vote to leave the European Union and was projected to be almost 1 percentage point lower than the baseline in 2017; a baseline which assumed that the United Kingdom would stay in the European Union. The accuracy of the central forecast for 2016 was reasonable and we all watched carefully to see what then happened.

That said, the substantive part of the economic impact of an exit from the EU single market was on the long run, what we might think of as the move from one pattern of trading relationships to a view about the new pattern of those relationships. This question formed the focus of most analysis because the empirical relationship between growth and trade is well established, such that a reduction in overall trade seems likely to imply a reduction in economic growth relative to the world in which there is no change in the overall level of trade. Note that this is an example of a *conditional* forecast. No one is saying that growth will be negative in the future without qualification. It is simply that, compared to any other view we may hold about the future state of the economy, one with significantly less trade is likely to have lower economic growth, at least for a while. To be clear the *unconditional* forecast predicts the date at which you will die, the *conditional* one says that if you smoke you will die a number of years earlier.

More important than any point forecast is the need to provide distributions that capture the measured extent of our uncertainty about forecasts, which we tend to term risk. The unmeasured uncertainty is usually called Knightian uncertainty, and we will return to this a little later. The way that forecast risk is estimated is that the set of errors from previous forecasts can be used to project a measure of the likely errors from the current most likely forecast path. Even a projection of normal times ahead would have a corridor of uncertainty around it, and so when we combine a lower expected rate of growth with the distribution of measurable possible outcomes, which is what we can calculate from previous episodes of economic news, a larger fraction of that distribution of likely outcomes will be below zero. If we think of recessions as periods of negative growth, then it is simply the projection of an increased possibility of growth outcomes below zero that represents any heightened possibility of recession.

EI.2   PLAYING WITH DICE

If you play with dice, think of forecasting as a game in the following way. Roll two standard dice that have one to six on their faces and note that you will get paid the amount rolled in pounds and now forecast what number will come up. The most likely number for two fair dice is seven, for which we can think of six combinations, which would then be your rational point forecast and so you might expect a £7 payoff from a dice throw and that is what you would be willing to pay to play the game. We can all agree that the correct forecast is seven, but we know even while making the forecast that we will be 'wrong' five-sixths of the time. The producer of the forecast knows that and the consumer must act accordingly. Two points follow. We cannot get at the underlying risk in our forecasts by asking even a thousand people for their point forecast because, if rational, they will all say seven. Secondly, the set of point forecasts superficially will look like people are herding around a particular view, therefore the producers of forecasts need to ask supplementary questions to evaluate the 'true' risk to our forecasts. As consumers we should not act on the point forecasts because we would tend to underestimate the extent of both risk and uncertainty.

Back to our game. Think of this return of £7 as akin to a normal times scenario. As already explained, the forecast is made in the full knowledge that it is much more likely to be wrong than right, but the question then facing us is the extent to which such a forecast may be useful; yes: because first it pins down the most likely number that may be useful for planning. We call this a measure of central tendency. If we want to plan more broadly we can allow for some small errors, which will be clearer if we say our forecast says that the dice will equal seven plus or minus two, which will be the case two-thirds of the time. Indeed, this fraction broadly corresponds to how much time the economy lives in normal rather than crisis times. The producer of the forecast has articulated central likelihood and a notion of how often we can expect normality rather than feast or famine. This statement may well be useful to consumers of forecasts.

The randomness implied by any one event means we cannot be at all sure what number will be returned following one draw (or shock), but under repeated trials we can form distributions that equal the likely probabilities of various events. What you will also value is the distribution or what we also call the risks to the forecast, as they will correspond to particular draws on the dice or equivalently economic shocks, or better still scenarios, by which I mean an articulated story about economics events such as oil prices, lending conditions, confidence or monetary conditions. Even then the impact of the change in a particular variable on the economic outlook depends on the shock. An unanticipated increase in oil prices may result from growth to world demand or the imposition of supply constraints on production. In the former case, the oil price change is endogenous to higher levels of growth in the world and may not signal an economic slowdown. But in the latter case, firms and households may have to reduce demand in order to budget for the higher costs of oil.

Now if we were to take the view that an economic cost (or tax) were to come along and this meant that it would cost you £3 of whatever you rolled, you would then forecast that the return from the game would only be £4 (i.e. £7–£3) and so the probability of a negative return has increased from 0 to 1/12. The forecasts of the impact of exiting the European Union, or indeed any view about a deteriorating economic outlook, reflected exactly that thought experiment and although we might expect worse returns overall, and as a result there was now a possibility of a negative return (or recession), we still might get lucky and the dice might fall favourably.

Another way we can play this game is to increase the variance without changing the expectation. This can be achieved by having one or more dice with zeros, positive and negative numbers; for example, two zeros, –2, –1, +1 and +2 would have an expected value of zero but also raise the variance of possible returns. Clearly in this case forecast errors will tend to be higher, but we would still not change our model expectation. What we would need to do is to think as producers how we can explain that forecasts are likely to have larger errors without necessarily being treated as failures and as consumers how we should react to these more uncertain times.

It is quite obvious that we cannot know the future, but it is also quite obvious that we cannot afford not to think and plan for the future. Projections about future states of the world depend on a combination of information and models, which are essentially devices for turning that unstructured information into a view. Even if we make the most extreme assumptions and assume that all relevant information is free, we would still not say that any structural view is anything other than a false or incorrect depiction of the world that will transpire. So any set of forecasts need to be treated with care, particularly when they are used to inform policy. Forecasts can be used or abused but they need to be made. How we should treat the falsity of forecasts is the subject to which I now turn.

E1.3   ARE FORECAST ERRORS BAD?

The implicit assumption made by many is that forecast accuracy is the overwhelming metric by which to judge the forecasting process. That is, in my view, an erroneous assumption. There are a number of value functions we might employ to assess the worth of a single or series of forecasts and only in some specific circumstances are we solely interested in minimising forecast errors – by which we mean the difference between the projection and the outcome – alone.

Let us first imagine that all forecast errors – whether small or large – lead to a loss in value, or utility. Let us further suppose that larger errors lead to a greater loss than smaller errors, whilst it is true in this formulation that no forecast errors will lead to no loss in utility. When there is a lack of perfect foresight, one may then not know quite what one would prefer between a large number of small errors or a small number of large errors.

However, the recent discussion about economic forecasts seems to me to be about large errors, with the implication that small errors are not terribly significant. This kind of reasoning is reflected in the Bank of England's inflation target, which imposes a penalty when there are large errors in outcomes (rather than forecasts) of 1 percentage point or more. In such a case the Governor of the Bank will write a letter of explanation to the Chancellor, which is published. But in the case of small errors, there is no obvious punishment at all. If we want models that concentrate on predicting large errors, which are rare, then we have to think of models that may not deal very well with the day-to-day or mundane. Ultimately the choice depends on the social welfare function. But one can imagine a world in which policymakers are told to avoid extreme events in all circumstances, which is quite different from the current imperative. Indeed crisis management may be the true policy calling of central banks.

If we are simply worried about extreme outcomes, one is quickly into the world of min-max, which is not so much about consistently high forecast accuracy but about minimising the losses from the maximum forecast error. The errors we care about are only the large ones in this world and policymakers will be acting on indicators of elevated levels of risk alone. This approach may not mitigate day-to-day risk very much and may even induce policy inspired fluctuations. Paul Samuelson wrote, 'to prove that Wall Street is an early omen of movements still to come in GNP, commentators quote economic studies alleging that market down-turns predicted four out of the last five recessions. That is an under-statement. Wall Street indexes predicted nine out of the last five recessions! And its mistakes were beauties'. If it is hard to predict with any degree of certainty the most likely throw of a dice at seven, it seems to me that it is several orders of magnitude harder to predict when we will throw a double six or double one.

Another possibility is that the direction of the forecast error might matter. When scrambling to get to Kings Cross for a train, the loss inflicted from being five minutes early is not the same as being five minutes late. The forecast error direction might well matter more than the strict size of the error. In this case one would prefer ten minutes early to one minute late. That one might prefer being more wrong to being less wrong can seem odd but is perfectly sensible given the nature of our preferences. The direction of error might also matter from the perspective of a trader on the financial markets who may take a position based on whether a particular economic indicator, such as non-farm payrolls, comes out above or below market expectations. Note that these market expectations themselves are produced from surveys of forecasts from professional economists. A trader, though, will make money if she has placed herself on the right side of the surprise. It matters little how close her view is to the outcome, only whether they are on the same side of the surprise as the market release.

Many studies concentrate on whether forecasts make money for a portfolio. These studies are moving away from statistical assess-ment to financial returns, which may be more concerned with the classification for forecasts in a non-parametric manner, such as a contingency table of whether the forecasts and outcomes tend to be the same side of surprise more often than we might expect by chance. Furthermore in this case, financial returns will depend on the costs of carrying a portfolio and the execution costs of a trade, which will encompass market liquidity. In other words the attitudes to forecast errors are state dependent. A small loss may not matter unless it takes the fund into bankruptcy and a large loss might be absorbed if there is sufficient capital. Even Keynes, writing in 1938, realised that trading on economic forecasts and information about firms may not always lead to high returns: 'we have not proved able to take much advantage of a general systematic movement out of and into ordinary shares as a whole at different phases of the trade cycle'.

This kind of problem might be the case in the policy world as well from time to time. If forecasts represent a game between the producer of forecasts and their consumers, in which convincing the latter may be an important part of the former's value function, things can get complicated very quickly, as we shall now consider.

EI.4   FORECASTING AND GIVING ADVICE

We may be fortunate to have a consensus view on the most likely outcome and this may come from the dice story I have outlined, but how should a rational agent 'consume' this advice? I shall suggest that simple theory tends to say that we should be wary of the motivation of those who forecast at the extreme and that we should still put weight on the central case. Although this book is about how central banks act, of ten in response to forecast and their errors, we are also quite accustomed to the entertaining spectator sport of economists disagreeing, often in very strong terms. However, the lead up to the EU referendum vote introduced to the public the rather strange sight of economists coming together nearly as one. The consensus was rather clear. The long-run central case was that reorienting trade and capital flows away from our largest trading partners in the EU would tend to reduce output in the long and short run. I do not want to go into the mechanics of these forecasts here but want to assess the problem from that of the consumer.

Actually like many contrary-minded people, I am often wary of the consensus as it may turn out to be misleading. Experts may tend to offer advice that favours the *status quo* because there is little substantive evidence in favour of an altered state of nature. They may also herd around one opinion because they do not want to be seen as outliers from their professional colleagues or because they have not been able to develop a truly independent view; either of these possibilities may lead to what economists call an informational cascade in which private information that may be valuable is not made public. Ideally, we would like forecasters' private information to be decanted into the public space so that we can benefit from the available views and act accordingly.

Some may think that all or some of the experts may also all be lying to us in order to gain some advantage later or are motivated by their own private returns from the choices of forecast consumers. We shall concentrate shortly on the incentives to influence consumers. But first we might dismiss the economic consensus on at least one of three grounds: (i) that experts are too risk averse; or (ii) short-sighted; or (iii) have formed a mendacious conspiracy. In the face of such possible biases, can yet more economic analysis help us again? Even if the signal from the experts is clear, the problem then is how we consume it. As members of the public, we may have pretty much one answer or signal, but before acting on it we have to decide how to treat any biases.

Assuming that all the economists who have provided various analyses want their advice to be heeded, they may also have tailored their advice so as to maximise the probability that the advice will be used by amplifying the signal: thinking that it is better to exaggerate the impact on the up or downside so that people will understand the qualitative stance on 'good' or 'bad' more easily; for example, to influence a trader, rather than forecasting a small surprise in the non-farm payrolls we might have to forecast a big surprise so as to outweigh her natural suspicions or uncertainties in the forecasts produced. An extreme view may be a cleaner signal.

If economists wished to influence opinion in this manner, the set of published views on either side would then actually become more dispersed as economists would exaggerate their claims in order to get more attention. Those making forecasts in the tail of the distribution are thus taking a very strong position, as they are putting a lot of weight on an unlikely scenario. If this happened there is further, more subtle impact. The increased polarisation of opinion on the impact of a particular event will then lead to increased uncertainty over the future, as rational agents will today attach some possibility to either extreme states. Accordingly we would (almost) certainly observe an increase in uncertainty as these two regimes tussle out the consequences of a given policy for the United Kingdom. Uncertainty itself then may lead to some delay in both consumption and investment, which may not be completely resolved until the episode and the policy shock have worked their way through the system.

The disinterested yet rational economist then has another choice. Let us suppose that whatever forecast or advice she wishes to publish, she wants the output consequences to be minimised. She will know that her advice may not be followed and that the other side may win the day. So she may have to change her advice in order to militate against the costs of her advice being ignored. How does she do this? She forecasts away from the extreme and reduces the range of possible outcomes. Our sensible economist wants to reduce uncertainty because she does not want to impart a shock on the economy as rational agents respond first to uncertainty and then to the expectation of a large change in circumstance. The public then might be best choosing the consensus when accepting advice: if the economists were truly disinterested in the results of an episode one way or the other, they would not wish to exaggerate the consequences because that would by itself negatively impact on the economy. We as the public should, in the absence of an ability to referee or replicate the analysis produced, be most wary of the outliers or extremes on either side. Perhaps the truly contrary thing in terms of the economics and the referendum is to agree with the remaining 'trimmed' consensus; discard the extremes and place weight on the central view.

E1.5 THE MODEL AS TIME MACHINE

NIESR has been developing its analysis of economic prospects and the causes of change since its establishment in 1938, but this process was heightened with the publication of the *National Institute Economic*

Review in 1959. By November 1963 forecasts of GDP started to be published and since then there has been an intense quarterly effort from economists running models, assessing data, understanding deviations of outcomes from expectations and applying dollops of judgement. When the output is brought together, as in other comparable organisations, NIESR staff start to make some sense of what has happened and think about what might happen. Even though many of our thoughts may not come to pass, like nightmares or dreams, it is quite necessary to think through the future using models.

An economic model is a parsimonious and, by definition, imperfect reflection of reality. It might be derived from first principles and respect economic theory, or it might be a set of relationships that capture observations and derive from empirical observation. The former and the latter are sometimes barely on speaking terms, but however we derive those relationships in a model, they collectively describe our view of how the world works. A forecaster, and perhaps with her judgement, would then crank that model into an unknowable future and would trace a number of possible futures: some more likely than others.

The economic forecast is thus ultimately an experiment in time travel not much different from those outlined by authors such as H. G. Wells, Ray Bradbury or Douglas Adams. The forecast allows the economist to articulate a future state of the world where each macroeconomic variable is consistent with every other macroeconomic variable. A good forecaster will articulate a large number of possible states of the world but where each set of macroeconomic variables is consistent with each other. All measurable scenarios will give us our fan chart of possible outcomes, so as well as an artificial universe, the modeller is inventing parallel universes. Think of a set of statements about output, inflation, exchange rates, productivity, unemployment and asset prices which are all consistent with each other in each possible state of the world; even better if we can incentivise different groups of modellers to articulate their model-consistent views of the world so that the genuine uncertainty we have about models and data can be reduced somewhat by more information.

The problem for the evaluation of forecasts arises because from the perspective of today, many possible states might obtain tomorrow, but when we get to that tomorrow only one state will have been obtained. That will mean that a forecast comprising many states will tend to look as though it is 'wrong'. As already outlined we know this very well: forecast accuracy does not imply the absence of forecast errors. One can go further because we not only expect less than perfect forecast accuracy when forecasting, we might actually welcome that; there are three broad reasons: first, if we collectively use information efficiently all that is left to explain the future is what we do not now know, and because we do not now know it, the future will be unknown and a surprise, or what economists call 'news'. Secondly, if we use the forecast to plan and set policy in order to minimise the worst expectations that will arise from our forecast, we will change the future. And the forecast will turn out, perhaps thankfully, to have a large error induced by our own policy actions.

Finally, and most importantly, we want to use the forecast errors to understand the news that has accrued since we made our original forecast. Without the forecast, which is what we anticipate, we cannot decompose future outcomes into what was anticipated and what was news. The anticipated part reflects the projection of key interrelationships in future time. The error from that anticipation or news ought to allow us to understand the economic story behind the forecast error but with a set of stringent side constraints. So if consumption is higher than we expected given our path for income, wages and the supply of funds, we have to construct a story that explains higher consumption but also then does not then fail to explain the subsequent path of income, wages and the supply of loanable funds. The model does not allow completely free thinking, and like a crossword, the answer must fit the letters of previously identified clues. An economic model does not admit anarchy.

Wells, Bradbury nor Adams quite got our present, as their future, quite right. Equally, forecasters prior to the Great Recession did not either and they would not have expected to be quite right. But elements of truth are there and those elements are useful. Wells' vision of a society dominated by the young; Bradbury's point about small events in the past having large effects in future; and Adams' guide for hitchhikers is really a smartphone. In some cases it is too early to tell how inaccurate they are and it is the same with any recent economic forecast.

E1.6   CONCLUDING REMARKS

Academic macroeconomic forecasting transformed following the financial crisis of the previous decade. Research produced a greater emphasis on model and data uncertainties, a push for more and better quality macroeconomic data and consideration of new models better suited to gauging risk. Risk can be captured by the measurable. But by using surveys, digital web-scraping and measures of confidence researchers are also trying to get at what was previously unmeasured, the Knightian world. The production of forecasts now stresses risk and uncertainty. Within that risk and uncertainty we need to explain better the various scenarios, stories or states of nature that add up to our measures of risk or uncertainty. The consumption of forecasts should now do so as well.

It might ultimately be time to start thinking of economic forecasting as akin, at least in the first pass, to projection. The forecast is essentially projecting a snapshot, perhaps one that is slightly out of focus, onto another plane. The further we project the image, the less well defined it will tend to be. We might then ask why do we project? The simple answer is so that more can see. The projection gives us a scenario or set of scenarios to think hard about and evaluate policy options for, and also to discuss, debate and deliberate. And that might be just enough. Why forecast? So we can think about possible futures and plan accordingly.

Epilogue 2: Monetary Policy in Troubled Times

The blissful world of the 'Great Moderation' might return. But for now it has gone. We do not yet fully understand its fast-changing successor. Monetary policy needs to be guided by principles, above all the principle that Hippocrates' oath nearly stated – 'do no harm'.

Peter Sinclair and William Allen (2017)

E2.1 INTRODUCTION

Assessing the mix of monetary and fiscal policies is a regular feature of informed commentary.[1] The timeless issues relating to the framework for monetary and fiscal policy and their appropriate degree of co-ordination have been exposed by the COVID-19 crisis. I have previously argued that the sequence of arbitrary fiscal rules that have been formulated by successive governments in the past decade do not make much economic sense, as they do not match a well-defined social welfare criterion.[2] I have also argued that the framework for monetary policy needs a close examination after the experiences of the global financial crisis and nearly twenty-three years of operational independence of the Bank of England.[3]

In March 2020, the economy was engulfed in a crisis almost without parallel in peacetime, and we anticipated a fall in activity in the region of 15–25 per cent in the initial period of lockdowns.

---

[1] See 'Fiscal Policy after the Referendum', November 2016, 'Interest Rate Normalisation', August 2017 and 'Monetary and Fiscal Policy Options in the Event of a "No-Deal" Brexit', August 2019. A version of this essay appeared as Chadha, J. (2020). Commentary: Monetary Policy in Troubled Times. National Institute Economic Review.

[2] See 'Time for the UK's "Budgetarians" to Make Way for Some Proper Fiscal Policy', Vox-EU CEPR, 9 March 2020.

[3] See *Renewing Our Monetary Vows: Open Letters to the Governor of the Bank of England*, NIESR Occasional Paper, 58.

We were on the cusp of what proved to be the first of several severe contractions in output as the authorities were forced to shut down society to limit the death toll from the COVID-19 strain of the coronavirus. We faced the prospect of whether the duration of lockdowns might get longer, implying that the impact on the economy and the scarring that would leave would increase the case for fiscal response; the need for extensive monetary support was clear.

As was increasingly clear, the economic and social crisis we faced was grave and it was possible for the Bank of England to provide space for fiscal policy to support economic activity without succumbing to a permanent regime shift towards fiscal dominance. But the monetary policy response should not simply have been defined solely by as direct crisis management. It became essential that the Governor and the Chancellor reflect on a sensible exit strategy for monetary policy from extraordinary operations. Many of the measures must be temporary and clearly designed as such: they should be state-dependent and be withdrawn once the crisis is over.

As such, the Bank of England faces a formidable challenge. From the first day in office on 16 March 2020, the new governor has been confronted with an imbalance between the demands on his institution to support the economy and its apparent capacity to meet that challenge. While the main responsibility to manage the economic crisis lay with fiscal policy, monetary policy should provide as much support as it can without undermining prospects for long-run price and financial stability. The problem is that with limited orthodox monetary space, given the size of the shock, there is an increasing pressure for the Bank to go further along the spectrum of choices towards even greater levels of unorthodoxy, which run a greater risk of undermining stability should institutional safeguards not be clearly established.

Unfortunately, at face value the Bank seems limited in its available response in conventional terms. Unlike in previous economic downturns, the bank cannot cut Bank Rate by several hundred basis points. Indeed, it has been clear for many years now that the Bank's capacity to support the economy through conventional monetary stimulus is much diminished. And whatever remained of the conventional monetary ammunition may have been exhausted, with rates seemingly at the floor and asset purchases resumed.

There will now be pressure to do more. The Bank will have to explore every nook and cranny of the monetary armoury to find new ways to nurse the economy through the crisis. With the Chancellor pressing ahead with a 'whatever it costs' strategy there will be a call on the Bank to do 'whatever it takes' to support that effort, which in practice means closer monetary-fiscal coordination and indeed a period of potential fiscal domination of the monetary economy.

Rules need to be agreed upon around the operational framework and regime for the Bank of England so that it will be able to respond to the next crisis, or even the next lockdown but also play a role in nurturing the economy back to health. This framework must then be endorsed and backed by elected politicians to allow the bank to go back to the business of delivering monetary and financial stability.

In this short epilogue I outline the guiding principles for monetary and fiscal policy in this crisis, the case for a dominant and substantial role for fiscal policy, a sliding scale of choices for the Bank of England that may have implications for the monetary settlement and a discussion of the case for helicopter money. I conclude by reiterating the case for retaining not only a clear nominal anchor consistent with price stability but also for a careful withdrawal of monetary policy from the arena of political choices over resource allocations in the presence of market failures.

E2.2   GUIDING PRINCIPLES

The economy is being used as an instrument to control the spread of COVID-19. Mass lockdowns across the world have been deployed as a way of limiting the spread of this virus; the United Kingdom started its lockdown on 23 March 2020. The COVID-19 economic crisis introduces what has been called radical uncertainty,[4] as we do not

---

[4] See Kay and King (2020).

know that much about its incidence or duration, but we are assuming that it is likely to be temporary but persistent. Accordingly, our analysis is based on that narrative. Unlike the 'usual' causes of economic fluctuations, this contraction does not result directly from monetary-fiscal-regulatory laxity, and so providing more complete insurance from public policy is not subject to the problem of extensive moral hazard. Indeed, in large part the economic crisis is the instrument of policy in guarding the nation's health. The implication then is that large-scale temporary monetary and fiscal support must be supplied. But who does what?

The chancellor's fiscal policy has to decide upon the quantum of risk that the economy faces that it cannot insure itself from, and then the overall level of resources to be transferred across the private sector by taxes and to future generations by debt issuance. It is not so much a question of whether there is a discretionary fiscal response but how much. The key point is that fiscal policy has to consider an actual transfer of resources across households and time that are either backed by current and/or future taxes. Our current estimates suggest that around a quarter of the economic loss might be met by the current strategy at HMT and there is room to do more. However, some remaining space might be conserved should further lockdowns be required to deal with the return of the virus or a mutation.

It is then a question for the Bank of England to decide whether that quantum of risk and resource transfer from fiscal policy requires any changes in the stance of monetary and financial policies. To that, as ever, there is the question of using short-run flexibility subject to the constraint of maintaining credibility or reputation, which is a critical intangible public sector asset. Indeed, it is typically found that aligning policies to people's long-run expectations of that institution's behaviour make short-run polices more effective, as they avoid problems associated with time inconsistency.

In confronting economic risk and radical uncertainty, of the manner in which COVID-19 has revealed it, fiscal policy must be prepared to revise its plans regularly in light of news about the spread of the virus and the economic impact here and overseas. It is also a sensible moment to establish more clearly a long-run objective to build up the net worth of the public sector balance sheet, alongside a commitment to sustainable levels of public debt within an institutional structure that provides regularly scheduled policy planning and projections on the path of the primary fiscal surplus and debt stock.

E2.3   FISCAL POLICY

In recent times, following a shock, in order to support the economy's adjustment to its long-run equilibrium, the main lever to stabilise economic fluctuations has been monetary policy. This has relied on deploying movements in Bank Rate or operations in the money market to influence longer-term interest rates to bring forward or defer expenditure. But the COVID-19 crisis has brought fiscal policy to the forefront of the policy imperative. There are broadly five reasons why we ought to focus mainly on fiscal policy in the first instance and deploy it in an active manner:

(1) The lockdown is an economic instrument that is directed at controlling the spread of COVID-19. Much of the market economy has thus been placed in a state of near suspended animation to limit the potential for a sharp increase in the virus infections through the domestic and global population, subject to the availability of health care services;

(2) The lockdown reduces the overall labour supply, but while there is excess labour supply in some areas such as the recreation, travel and restaurant sectors, there is a shortage in others, for example, in healthcare, agriculture and childcare. The state, as in wartime, could help divert labour to areas where required and provide basic training for necessary skills development;

(3) The economic shock more obviously affects those households who cannot work on a sustained basis in a remote manner, many of those who are self-employed and those without sufficient savings to sustain expenditure patterns for necessities. This will tend to affect those in the lower income deciles, and this argues for a considerable effort on redistributive policies;

(4) Using the list of identified projects at the National Infrastructure Commission, we should be aiming to bring forward public investment as soon as lockdowns are eased. If we are heading for a sequence of lockdowns, then any projects that can be completed quickly, at the local authority level or for social housing, should be deployed;

(5) Finally, when the monetary policy space is constrained and when demand falls so rapidly, it seems very likely that fiscal multipliers are quite large – that is, for every pound spent the impact on the economy will not be crowding out private sector activity.

E2.4   MONETARY POLICY OPTIONS[5]

The Bank of England faces a formidable challenge. The case for a powerful monetary stimulus to nurse the economy through the current crisis is overwhelming. This Monetary Policy Committee (MPC) cannot cut interest rates by several hundred basis points as predecessors might have done. There was relatively little conventional monetary ammunition before the COVID-19 crisis, and much of what remained has already been exhausted.

Yet, monetary policy cannot sit this slump out and must do whatever it can in support of the government's crisis response. There are three sets of issues to resolve: first, what can still be done within the conventional toolkit; second, what can be done in the space of formal monetary-fiscal co-ordination; and third, what must be done once the crisis is over, which I consider in Section E2.5.

E2.4.1   Exhausting What Remains of Conventional Space

There are three basic options open to the Monetary Policy Committee to inject additional stimulus if it is required: further asset purchases, forward guidance and negative rates. None look particularly promising, in terms of delivering a sufficient level of stabilisation, but all may have to be explored.

---

[5] This section draws heavily on Richard Barwell, Jagjit Chadha and Mick Grady (2020) NIESR Occasional Paper, 59.

There is scope to stimulate the economy further through large-scale asset purchases, although long-term risk-free rates are already low. Purchases of riskier assets offer the possibility of more leverage on aggregate demand and might prove powerful in a crisis in which credit and equity risk premia can widen significantly. However, clarity on objectives and a discussion on governance are paramount in the design of any asset purchase scheme. The questions to think about are how much government debt should be bought by the central bank; how large should its balance sheet grow; and with what level of risk? Even though quantitative easing has been in place in the United Kingdom since 2009, we have still not developed good answers to these questions.

There is little additional monetary space to be found in what has become known as forward guidance – that is, communication that reflects an orthodox reaction to events or news. The only way to ease the stance through communication is via a clear commitment to change that reaction function. That in turn requires a credible and transparent commitment device, preferably a target path for the price level, or failing that an average inflation-targeting regime. A published path for the policy instruments that explains likely responses in different states of the world, would also help.

There are valid concerns about whether maintaining negative rates for an extended period will ultimately prove counterproductive. But there is evidence from the Euro Area of some efficacy. Policymakers may need to examine the literature on the reversal rate – the rate at which lower interest rates lead to a contraction in bank lending rather than an increase – a little more carefully. But even if they are still not convinced, there may well be an argument for negative interest rates for reserves to deal with large shocks and disconnecting the one-to-one exchange rate between cash and deposits, so that holding cash becomes relatively costly.

E2.4.4.2   Formal Monetary–Fiscal Co-ordination

Whatever remains of the conventional monetary space is likely to prove insufficient. More will need to be done. The Chancellor is pursuing the right strategy of 'whatever it costs' to support the economy, but that in turn requires a significant, albeit so far quite sustainable, increase in government debt to finance critical support for the economy. In this crisis, greater co-ordination between the monetary and fiscal authorities is justified, with the Bank taking the steps to create and preserve fiscal space. There are a range of options on the table.

Direct yield curve control would place a limit or target on bond yields. It provides a robust and transparent regime for preserving fiscal space, and has the added virtue of signalling the transition of responsibility for demand management to the fiscal authority. Ideally, the purpose of a yield cap would be to suppress any contractionary increase in bond yields given a shift in rate expectations or the term premium (due to higher net issuance), but in a crisis it may keep a lid on rising sovereign credit and inflation risk premia, provided long-run credibility is maintained. As ever, the control of a price would rob it of its information content so it may become progressively harder to gauge financial risk and changes in inflation expectations.

Alternatively, fiscal space can be secured by working directly on quantities – that is, the Bank could engage in some form of monetary financing. By committing to purchase government bonds in the magnitude issued, under strict conditions and only for a limited period, a central bank can support proper market functioning and prevent an unwarranted tightening in financial conditions. The announcement of extended use of Ways and Means on 9 April 2020 was simply the deployment of an overdraft facility that limits liquidity disruption in sterling money markets, as unanticipated debt issuance is so large. At face value the announcement does not constitute monetary financing, not least because it is being carried out within the Bank's inflation-targeting remit. However, there are some missing parts: the absence of a statement on the overall quantity of the overdraft on this facility and on its duration. It would also be normal for an exchange of letters between the Chancellor and the Governor to set these out, as well as how decisions on future of use of the Ways and Means facility will work.[6]

Finally, there is the possibility of a mythical 'helicopter drop'. Governments, not central banks, have the experience, infrastructure and remit of distributing cash to the general public. But the Bank can engineer a helicopter drop through a credible commitment that monetary financing will be permanent. Purchases of government debt, whether made in the secondary market or in a more unorthodox manner via primary purchases, would remain on the Bank's balance sheet indefinitely. This is the most extreme of the three options, and carries the greatest risk to monetary stability as it states that the nominal anchor will drag. I will return to this question in the next section.

Within the range of these options, the obvious next step is yield curve control as it is close to quantitative easing in that a price is set rather than a quantity delivered, but both intend to influence long-term bond prices. Indeed, a case can be made for yield curve control on the grounds that it makes more sense to control bond prices than to control the quantity of purchases in the hope of influencing bond prices. However, if the commitment to a target were to be tested by market participants – in the same manner as a commitment to an exchange rate peg – then the policy may ultimately converge on monetary financing.

E2.4.4.3   Quantitative Easing, Monetary Financing and Helicopter Money

In an earlier generation of macroeconomic models, it was hard to find a direct role for money to affect the economy as it provided a veil over real decisions to spend or invest.[7] Certainly in these models money, per se, did not constitute net wealth for the private sector. As models developed and incorporated financial frictions it was possible to show

---

[6] At the time of writing, 20 April 2020, no such decision or letter had been exchanged.

[7] Jagjit Chadha, Luisa Corrado and Sean Holly (2014) explore this decomposable property.

that the relaxation of lending conditions, which lead to the build-up of debt, might amplify economic fluctuations. To the extent that the supply of funds was not well pinned down by movements in policy rates, there was a case for alternate operating procedures. Accordingly, when policy rates were constrained, other ways to influence monetary and financial conditions had to be found.

We cannot very easily draw a distinction between changes in Bank Rate and the policies followed at the zero lower bound of bond purchases, in so far as bond or asset purchases are an attempt to alleviate monetary and financial conditions in the same manner as movements in Bank Rate. In this case, the steps are that the fiscal policymaker has made some decision to issue debt. Depending on the capacity of markets to absorb this debt, the resultant bond prices may not be quite where the central bank wants them to be, given the stance of monetary policy or constraints on policy rates. In this case government debt is bought from the non-bank financial sector on a temporary but probably long-term basis. Note that the debt is funded and future taxes are still expected to be remitted to pay these debts. Debt issuance that is not funded by taxes does not have a very promising history and Sargent (1982) tells the sorry tale of the causes of four hyperinflations.

Monetary financing is the direct purchase of debt by the central bank. It bypasses the transmission mechanism in the real economy and simply hands unfunded resource allocation or tokens (money) to the Treasury, which competes with private sector allocations. There may be no intention of raising tax to meet these overdrafts and the bonds are held permanently by the central bank with an increase in its balance sheet. If the private sector thought that these tokens were claims on real resources then they would have some stimulatory effect on the economy (see Buiter, 2014). Indeed, if one took the view that households would always demand central bank money, were it issued in ever larger quantities and placed a positive value on it related to the claims on output, then it could always be relied on to boost output, even in a helicopter drop. But the prospects for a stable demand for central bank money in the presence of a large or repeated deployment of this tool seem to be strictly limited. The magnitude of any stimulatory effect seems unlikely to be much larger than a more standard form of debt issuance with QE.[8]

E2.5   AFTER THE CRISIS: RESUMING NORMAL SERVICE

Even this crisis will eventually pass. When that happens, it will be essential that the Governor and the Chancellor revisit the gaps that have been exposed in the fiscal and monetary framework. The first order of business is to devise and state a credible exit strategy from the extraordinary policy measures that will have been taken during the crisis.[9] Some measures are harder to exit than others. An orderly retreat from yield curve control – by slowly relaxing the grip and widening the tolerance band around the target – seems easier to engineer than scaling back the quantum of purchases. The device of making the exit from extraordinary measures contingent on a return to normality – that is state dependent – is one such route. However, we have not yet returned to the previous norm after the financial crisis, and this means the permanent and the temporary are very hard to disentangle.

In terms of initial conditions for this crisis, the fundamental problem the bank faces is a lack of monetary space. There is one obvious solution: raise the inflation target to 4 per cent to offset the decline in equilibrium real interest rates, but that threatens normal notions of what constitutes price stability with prices then doubling every seventeen to eighteen years. There is also a danger that any immediate shift in the nominal anchor may be misunderstood as an expedient device during a crisis, and as we do not want to dislodge stable price expectations and the contribution to regularised exchange that affords, any decision to move it must wait.

---

[8] Richard Harrison and Ryland Thomas (2019) on this point.
[9] By exit strategy here I mean strictly the monetary and financial measures and not what common discussion has linked to the exit from lockdowns, which is quite a different form of exit strategy.

Finally, the Bank itself needs an exit strategy from the so-called only game in town trap, in which the central bank and its balance sheet are the answers to every problem – from infrastructure to greening the economy. There must be a return to the narrow focus of monetary and financial stability. The pursuit of broader social objectives and the conduct of industrial and credit policy must be left to the politicians.

E2.6   CONCLUSION

The modern, recent history of monetary policymaking in the United Kingdom has unfolded over three key events: exit from the European Exchange Rate Mechanism in September 1992; the election of 'New Labour' in 1997 with Gordon Brown as Chancellor; and the global financial crisis of 2007–2008. The first led directly to the adoption of an explicit inflation target for monetary policy in October 1992; the second led to the adoption of operational independence for the Bank of England's Monetary Policy Committee (MPC) in pursuit of that target; and the third exposed the limitations of single-minded inflation targeting pursued solely via manipulations in Bank Rate. With the terrible events associated with the spread of COVID-19, the UK monetary authorities have an opportunity to move the dial further on to adopt instruments that increase the space for monetary policy but also respect the boundary between the political choices of the state and the technical matters of ensuring monetary financial stability in the face of shocks.

At the same time, we need to ensure that sensible commitments about the long run are not lost. One way to frame the policy innovations over the past decade or so is that we have been trying to nurture a fragile economy back to normal. The patient simply cannot take normal stresses and strains. The global financial crisis had the capacity to bring about a decade of prolonged depression; that it did not is a testament to extraordinary monetary policies. In time, the pressing issues will be to help the government redefine the numerical objective for monetary stability: being clearer about the links between the MPC and Financial Policy Committee as bodies both affecting monetary and financial conditions. Think hard about communication as part of the instrument toolkit and finally contribute to the measurement and understanding of the new economy. Indeed, the best answer of all might be for the Governor to call for an external review of the Bank's Remit and Objectives and use that to refocus on the bread and butter of central banking in the long run, while managing the crisis in whatever-it-takes mode until then. Let's do no harm.

A Final Word

Over the course of the twentieth century, economic policy increasingly took on the obligation of maximising household welfare subject to available resources in the presence of markets that need regulation, information, co-ordination and the ready supply of public goods. Within that large set of policies – ranging from education to defence – which manage a complex economy that sits itself within a world of exchange and trade, what do central bankers seek to do? The imperative to stabilise is clear. This is not so much a problem about exploration, experimentation and innovation but about creating conditions under which plans can be formulated and exercised with some degree of certainty that monetary and financial exchange will be safeguarded.

The economy is a term that sums up a vast number of monetary and non-monetary choices by households, firms and government bodies in the pursuit of some notion of welfare maximisation. The money minders are a shy race. They neither want to tell people how to spend their time, nor what goods or services should be developed or bought; nor can they seek particularly to promote technical progress, or what is usually called productivity. The waves of knowledge and know-how by which an economy grows and contracts are neither under the control of central banks nor especially predictable. It would therefore be quite wrong to seek to control all of the variation in income and domestic outcomes, much of which in any case will flow from the specific circumstance of household skill levels, the networks to which they belong, the places and spaces in which they live and sheer dumb luck.

As the money minder builds monetary and financial bridges and all the roads linking the transactions we choose to effect, she only really needs to know the quantity or weight of that transaction traffic.

The money minder must pay attention to the evolution of the economy and compare how we used to live with how we plan to live; she cannot and should not seek to control the origin or destination of each journey. Decisions on monetary policy are not designed to foster permanent changes in behaviour but to prevent the flow of information and the build of financial claims from throwing the economy into problematic volatilities in the patterns of employment, inflation and income. The responsibility for maintaining monetary and financial stability limits the scope for central bank policymaking and public pronouncement but should also limit the questions asked of it by politicians. It is the latter, in a democracy, who must respond to inequity, provide insurance and ask how much of risk is to be transferred across those currently alive and those yet to be born. The money minders want to ensure that all those generations will then simply be able to affect trade and exchange to the full extent; their judgements on the new events that constantly unfold will hinge on theory and practice that will continue to build on parables, explore trade-offs and respect lags.

References

Alesina, A. and Summers, L. H., (1993). Central Bank Independence and Macroeconomic Performance: Some Comparative Evidence, *Journal of Money, Credit and Banking*, 25, pp. 151–162.

Allen, F. and D. Gale, (2007). *Understanding Financial Crises*, Clarendon Lectures in Finance, Oxford: Oxford University Press.

Allen, F. and D. Gale, (2007). *Understanding Financial Crises*, Oxford: Oxford University Press.

Allen, W., Chadha, J. S., and Turner, P. (2021). Commentary: Quantitative Tightening: Protecting Monetary Policy from Fiscal Encroachment. *National Institute Economic Review*, 257, 1–8. doi:10.1017/nie.2021.27

Ayres, C. E., (1946). The Impact of the Great Depression on Economic Thinking, *American Economic Review*, 36(2), pp. 112–125.

Bagehot, W., ([1873] 1898). *Lombard Street: A Description of the Money Market*, New York: Charles Scriber's Sons.

Bagehot, W., (1873). *Lombard Street: A Description of the Money Market*, London: Henry S. King and Co.

Barro, R. J., (1979). Money and Price Level under the Gold Standard, *Economic Journal*, 89, pp. 13–33.

Barro, R. J. and D. B. Gordon, (1983). Rules, Discretion and Reputation in a Model of Monetary Policy, *Journal of Monetary Economics*, 12(1), pp. 101–121.

Barwell, R. and Chadha, J. S. (2019) (eds.). *Renewing Our Monetary Vows: Open Letters to the Governor of the Bank of England*, National Institute of Economic and Social Research, Occasional Paper No 58.

Barwell, R., Chadha, J. S. and Grady, M. (2020). *Monetary Policy in Troubled Times: New Governor ... New Agenda*, National Institute of Economic and Social Research, Occasional Paper No 59.

Bean, C. R., (2004). Asset Prices, Financial Instability, and Monetary Policy, *American Economic Review*, 94(2), pp. 14–18.

Bernanke, B. S., (2003). A Perspective on Inflation Targeting: Why It Seems to Work, speech to the Annual Washington Policy Conference of the National Association of Business Economists, Washington, DC, 25 March.

Bernanke, B. S., (2004). The Great Moderation, speech to the Eastern Economic Association, Washington, DC, February 20, www.federalreserve.gov/boarddocs/speeches/2004/20040220.

Bernanke, B. S. and A. Blinder, (1988). Credit, Money and Aggregate Demand, *American Economic Review*, 78(2), pp. 435–439.

Bernanke, B., Reinhart, V. and B. Sack, (2004). Monetary Policy Alternatives at the Zero Bound: An Empirical Assessment, *Brookings Papers on Economic Activity*, 35(2), pp. 1–100.

Blinder, A. (1998). *Central Banking in Theory and Practice*, Cambridge, MA: MIT Press.

Bordo, M. D. and F. E. Kydland, (1992). The Gold Standard as a Rule, Federal Reserve Bank of Cleveland Working Paper, No. 9205, (March 1992).

Brainard, W. W., (1967). Uncertainty and the Effectiveness of Policy, *American Economic Review*, 57(2), pp. 411–425.

Breedon, F., J. S. Chadha and A. Waters, (2012). The Financial Market Impact of UK Quantitative Easing, *Oxford Review of Economic Policy*, 28(4), pp. 702–728.

Buiter, W. H. (2014). 'The Simple Analytics of Helicopter Money: Why It Works – Always', Economics Discussion Papers, No 2014-24, Kiel Institute for the World Economy.

Caglar, E., J. S. Chadha, J. Meaning, J. Warren and A. Waters, (2011). Central Bank Balance Sheet Policies: Three Views from the DSGE Literature, in J. S. Chadha and S. Holly (eds.) *Interest Rates, Prices and Liquidity*. Cambridge: Cambridge University Press, pp. 240–273.

Carlson, J. B., B. Craig, P. Higgins and W. R. Melick, (2006). *FOMC Communications and the Predictability of Near-Term Policy Decisions*, Cleveland: Federal Reserve Bank of Cleveland Economic Commentary.

Chadha, J. S. and N. Dimsdale, (1999). A Long View of Real Rates, *Oxford Review of Economic Policy*, 15(2), pp. 17–45.

Chadha, J. S. and S. Holly (ed.), (2011). *Interest Rates, Prices and Liquidity*, Cambridge: Cambridge University Press.

Chadha, J. S. and E. Newby, (2013). Midas, Transmuting All, into Paper: The Bank of England and the Banque de France during the Napoleonic Wars, Bank of Finland Discussion Paper, 20/2013 (also available as *Cambridge Working Paper in Economics*, CWPE1330).

Chadha, J. S. and C. Nolan, (2001). Inflation Targeting, Transparency and Interest Rate Volatility: Ditching Monetary Mystique in the UK, *Journal of Macroeconomics*, 23(3), pp. 349–366.

Chadha, J. S. and M. Perlman, (2014). Was the Gibson Paradox for Real? A Wicksellian Study of the Relationship between Interest Rates and Prices, *Financial History Review*, 21, pp. 139–163.

Chadha, J. S. and L. Sarno, (2002). Short- and Long-Run Price Level Uncertainty under Different Monetary Policy Regimes: An International Comparison, *Oxford Bulletin of Economics and Statistics*, 64(3), pp. 187–216.

Chadha, J. S. and P. Schellekens, (1999). Monetary Policy Loss Functions: Two Cheers for the Quadratic, Bank of England Working Paper No. 101.

Chadha, J. S., A. Clarke and P. Mortimer-Lee, (2007). Memorandum of Written Evidence Submitted to the Treasury Committee, www.publications.parliament .uk/pa/cm200607/cmselect/cmtreasy/299/299we21.htm.

Chadha, J. S., G. Corrado, L. Corrado and I. D. L. Buratta, (2021), The Role of Macroprudential Policy in Times of Trouble, bank of Portugal Working Paper, No. 3.

Chadha, J. S., L. Corrado and S. Holly, (2014). A Note on Money and the Conduct of Monetary Policy, *Macroeconomic Dynamics*, 18(08), pp. 1854–1883.

Chadha, J. S., L. Corrado, J. Meaning, and T. Schuler, "Monetary and fiscal complementarity in the Covid-19 pandemic", ECB Working paper No. 2588.

Chadha, J. S., L. Corrado and Q. Sun, (2010). Money, Prices and Liquidity Effects: Separating Demand from Supply, *Journal of Economic Dynamics and Control*, 34(9), pp. 1732–1747.

Chadha, J. S., P. Macmillan and C. Nolan, (2007). Independence Day for the 'Old Lady': A Natural Experiment on the Implications of Central Bank Independence, *Manchester School*, 75(3), pp. 311–327.

Chamberlin, G., (2009). The Housing Market and Household Balance Sheets, *Economic and Labour Market Review*, 3(9), pp. 24–33.

Checkland, S., (1983). *British Public Policy 1776–1939: An Economic, Social and Political Perspective*, Cambridge: Cambridge University Press.

Chrystal, A., J. Pearlman, P. N. Smith and S. Wright (eds.), (2016). *The UK Economy in the Long Expansion and Its Aftermath*, Cambridge: Cambridge University Press.

Clapham, J., (1944a). *The Bank of England: A History, Volume 1, 1694–1797*, Cambridge: Cambridge University Press.

Clapham, J., (1944b). *The Bank of England, A History: Volume 2, 1797–1914*, Cambridge: Cambridge University Press.

Clarida, R. and M. Gertler, (1997). *How the Bundesbank Conducts Monetary Policy*, in Romer, C. D. and Romer, D. H. (eds.) *Reducing Inflation: Motivation and Strategy*. Chicago: University of Chicago Press.

Clarida, R., M. Gertler and S. Gilchrist, (1999). The Science of Monetary Policy: A New Keynesian Perspective, *Journal of Economic Literature*, 37, pp. 1661–1707.

Collins, M., (1982). Unemployment in Interwar Britain: Still Searching for an Explanation, *Journal of Political Economy*, 90(2), pp. 369–379.

Coyle, C. and J. D. Turner, (2013). Law, Politics, and Financial Development: The Great Reversal of the UK Corporate Debt Market, *Journal of Economic History*, 73(3), pp. 810–846.

Coyle, D., (2014). *GDP: A Brief But Affectionate History – Revised and Expanded Edition*, Princeton, NJ: Princeton University Press.

Crockett, A. D., (2000). Marrying the Micro- and Macro-Prudential Dimensions of Financial Stability, Eleventh International Conference of Banking Supervisors.

Dasgupta, P., (2005). The Economics of Social Capital, A. C. Mills Lecture, delivered at the Annual Conference of Australian Economists, University of Sydney, September 2004.

Davies, H. (2000). Speech to Bond Market Association's Sixth Annual Legal and Compliance Conference, 26 October, www.fsa.gov.uk/Pages/Library/ Communication/Speeches/2000/sp62.shtml.

Dimsdale, N., S. Hills and R. Thomas, (2010). The UK Recession in Context: What Do Three Centuries of Data Tell Us? Bank of England Data Annex.

Dow, C., (1998). *Major Recessions – Britain and the World, 1920–1995*, Oxford: Oxford University Press.

The Economist, (1997). A Good Start, 10 May, p. 13.

Feavearyear, A. E., (1931). *The Pound Sterling : A History of English Money*, Oxford: Clarendon Press.

Feinstein, C. H., (1972). *Statistical Tables of National Income, Expenditure and Output of the UK, 1855–1965*, Cambridge: Cambridge University Press.

Feinstein, C. H., (ed.) (1983). *The Managed Economy: Essays in British Economic Policy and Performance since 1929*, Oxford: Oxford University Press.

Fischer, S., (1990). Rules versus Discretion in Monetary Policy, in Friedman, B. M. and Hahn, F. H. (ed.) *Handbook of Monetary Economics*, volume 2, chapter 21, pp. 1155–1184.

Freidman, M., (1959). *A Program for Monetary Stability*, New York: Fordham University Press.

Freidman, M., (1968). The Role of Monetary Policy, *American Economic Review*, 58(1), pp. 1–17.

Friedman, M., and A. J. Schwartz, (1963). *A Monetary History of the United States, 1867–1960*, Princeton, NJ: Princeton University Press for NBER.

Frisch, R., (1970). *From Utopian Theory to Practical Applications: The Case of Econometrics*, Lecture to the Memory of Alfred Nobel, June 17.

Fuhrer, J., (1997). Inflation/Output Variance Trade-Offs and Optimal Monetary Policy, *Journal of Money, Credit and Banking*, 29(2), pp. 214–234.

Gagnon, J., M. Raskin, J. Remache and B. Sack, (2010). Large-Scale Asset Purchases by the Federal Reserve: Did They Work?, *Economic Policy Review*, 17, pp. 41–59.

Gale, D., (1982). *Money in Equilibrium*, Cambridge: Cambridge University Press.

Gale, D., (2011). Liquidity and Monetary Policy, in Chadha and Holly (eds.) *Interest Rates, Prices and Liquidity*. Cambridge: Cambridge University Press.

George, E. (2002). *Interview*, Central Banking Publications, pp. 22–32, www .centralbanking.co.uk/pdfs/george.pdf.

Goetzmann, W. and G. Rouwenhorst, (2005). *The Origins of Value*, Oxford: Oxford University Press.

Gogol, N. (1835/2005). Diary of a Madman, in Nikolay Gogol, Robert Maguire (introducer) and Ronald Wilks (translator) *Diary of a Madman, the Government Inspector, and Selected Stories*. London: Penguin.

Goodhart, C. A. E., (2007). Whatever Became of the Monetary Aggregates?, *National Institute Economic Review*, 200, pp. 56–61.

Goodhart, C. A. E., (2008). The Future of Finance and the Theory That Underpins It, LSE Report, chapter 5, London School of Economics.

Goodhart, C. A. E. and A. D. Crockett, (1970). The Importance of Money, *Bank of England Quarterly Bulletin*, 10(2), pp. 159–198.

Green R. (1989). Real Bills Doctrine, in Eatwell J., Milgate M. and Newman P. (eds.) *Money: The New Palgrave*. London: Palgrave Macmillan.

Hall, R., (2009). The High Sensitivity of Economic Activity to Financial Frictions. *NBER mimeo*.

Harrison, R. and Thomas, R. (2019). 'Monetary Financing Interest-Bearing Money', Bank of England Staff Working Paper No 785.

Hawtrey, R. G., (1930). *Currency and Credit*, London: Longmans, Green and Company.

Hawtrey, R. G., (1932). *The Art of Central Banking*, London: Longmans, Green and Company.

Hawtrey, R. G., (1934). *The Art of Central Banking*, London: Longmans.

Hicks, J. R., (1937). Mr Keynes and 'Classics': A Suggested Interpretation, *Econometrica*, 5(2), pp. 147–159.

Hume, D., (1752/1987), Of Money, in *Of Money and Other Essays*, revised edition, Indianapolis: Liberty Fund.

Hume, D., ([1752] 1970). Of Money, in Rotwein, Eugene (ed.) *Writings on Economics*. Madison: University of Wisconsin Press.

Hume, D., (1777/1987). Essays Moral, Political, Literary, Part II, Essay III, *Of Money*. Indianapolis: Liberty Fund.

Joyce, M., A. Lasaosa, I. Stevens and M. Tong, (2010). The Financial Market Impact of Quantitative Easing. Bank of England Working Paper No. 393, pp. 1–44.

Kay, J. and King, M. A. (2020). *Radical Uncertainty: Decision-Making beyond the Numbers*, London: Norton.

Key, T., V. Paul, M. Weale and T. Wieladek, (2016). Property Income and the Balance of Payments, in Chrystal et al., pp. 111–130.

Keynes, J. M., (1923 [1932]). *Essays in Persuasion*, London: Norton.

Keynes, J. M., (1924). *Monetary Reform*, New York: Harcourt, Brace and Co.

Keynes, J. M., (1936). *The General Theory of Employment, Interest and Money*, New York: Harcourt, Brace and Co.

Kindleberger, C. P., (1984). *A Financial History of Western Europe*, London: George Allen and Unwin.

King, M. A. (1997). Changes in UK Monetary Policy, *Rules and Discretion in Practice, Journal of Monetary Economics*, 39, pp. 81–97.

King, M. A. (2002). No Money, No Inflation: The Role of Money in the Economy, *Bank of England Quarterly Bulletin*, 42, pp. 162–177.

King, M. A., (2010). Banking: From Bagehot to Basel, and Back Again, speech at the Second Bagehot Lecture, New York, Buttonwood Gathering, 25 October.

Kiyotaki, N. and J. H. Moore (2001). Evil Is the Root of All Money, *Clarendon Lecture in Economics*, Lecture 1 mimeo.

Krishnamurthy, A. and Vissing-Jorgensen, A., (2011). The Effects of Quantitative Easing on Long-Term Interest Rate. Northwestern University Working Paper, pp. 1–47.

Kydland, F. E. and E. C. Prescott, (1977). Rules Rather Than Discretion: The Inconsistency of Optimal Plans, *Journal of Political Economy*, 85(3), pp. 473–492.

Lawson, N., (1992). *The View from No. 11: Memoirs of a Tory Radical*, London: Bantam Press.

Leach, T., (2013). *The Last King of Lydia*, London: Atlantic Books.

Levenson, T., (2009). *Newton and Counterfeiters*, London: Faber and Faber.

Lewis, J. and J. Saleheen, (2016). Emerging Markets and Import Prices during the Long Expansion, in Chrystal et al., pp. 397–408.

Lucas, R. E., (1976). Econometric Policy Evaluation: A Critique, *Carnegie Rochester Conference Series*, 1, pp. 19–46.

Lucas, R. E., (1987). *Models of Business Cycles*, New York: Basil Blackwell.

Lucas, R. E., Jr., (1996). Nobel Lecture: Monetary Neutrality, *Journal of Political Economy*, 104, pp. 661–682.

Lucas, R., (1976). Econometric Policy Evaluation: A Critique, in K. Brunner and A. Meltzer (eds.), *The Phillips Curve and Labor Markets*. Carnegie-Rochester, Conference Series on Public Policy, pp. 19–46.

Matthews, R. C. O., (1968). Why Has Britain Had Full Employment since the War? *Economic Journal*, 78(311), pp. 555–569.

McCallum, B. T. (2002). Recent Developments in Monetary Policy Analysis: The Roles of Theory and Evidence, *FRB Richmond – Economic Review*, 88(1), pp. 67–96.

McLeay, M. and R. Thomas, (2016). UK Broad Money Growth in the Long Expansion 1992–2007: What Can It Tell Us about the Role of Money?, in Chrystal et al.

Meade, J. E., (1961). The Case for Variable Exchange Rates, *Three Banks Review*, 27, pp. 3–27.

Meier, A., (2009). Panacea, Curse, or Nonevent: Unconventional Monetary Policy in the United Kingdom. IMF Working Paper No. 9/163, pp. 1–48.

Middleton, R., (1985). *Towards the Managed Economy: Keynes, the Treasury and the Fiscal Debate of the 1930s*, London: Methuen and Company.

Milne, A. and J. A. Wood, (2016). An Old Fashioned Banking Crisis: Credit Growth and Loan Losses in the UK, 1997–2012, in Chrystal et al., pp. 210–243.

Mitchell, B. R., (1962). *Abstract of British Historical Statistics*, Cambridge: Cambridge University Press.

Modigliani, F. and Sutch, R., (1966). Innovations in Interest Rate Policy, *American Economic Review*, 52, pp. 178–197.

Moggridge, D. E., (1972). *British Monetary Policy: The Norman Conquest of $4.86*, Cambridge: Cambridge University Press.

Montesquieu, 1973 [1721]. *Persian Letters*. Translated with an introduction and notes by C. J. Betts, London: Penguin.

Morris, S. and H. S. Shin, (2005). Central Bank Transparency and the Signal Value of Prices, *Brookings Papers on Economic Activity*, 2(2), pp. 1–66.

Mundell, R. A., (1961). A Theory of Optimum Currency Areas, *American Economic Review*, 51(4), pp. 657–665.

Nickell, S., (2005). Why Has Inflation Been So Low since 1999?, presented at a meeting of the Bank of England Regional Agents.

Nordhaus, W. D., (1994). Marching to Different Drummers: Coordination and Independence in Monetary and Fiscal Policies, Cowles Foundation Discussion Papers No. 1067.

Peden, G. C., (1988). *Keynes, the Treasury and British Economic Policy*, Studies in Economic and Social History, Cambridge: Cambridge University Press.

Phillips, A. W., (1958). The Relation between Unemployment and the Rate of Change of Money Wage Rates in the United Kingdom, 1861–1957, *Economica*, 25(100), pp. 283–299.

Pigou, A. C., (1948). *Aspects of British Economic History, 1918–1925*, London: Macmillan and Company.

Poole, W., (1970). Optimal Choice of Monetary Policy Instruments in a Simple Stochastic Macro Model, *Quarterly Journal of Economics*, 84(2), pp. 197–216.

Popper, K., (1959). *The Logic of Scientific Discovery*, New York: Harper and Row.

Priestly, J. B., (1934). *English Journey*, London: Penguin.

Radford, R. A., (1945). The Economic Organisation of a P.O.W. Camp, *Economica*, 12(48), pp. 189–201.

Rawnsley, A., (2000). *Servants of the People: The Inside Story of New Labour*, London: Hamish Hamilton.

Rogoff, K., (1985). The Optimal Degree of Commitment to an Intermediate Target, *Quarterly Journal of Economics*, 100, pp. 1169–1189.

Rotemberg, J. and M. Woodford, (1997). An Optimization-Based Econometric Framework for the Evaluation of Monetary Policy, *NBER Macroeconomics Annual*, 12, pp. 297–346.

Samuelson, P. A., (1958). An Exact Consumption-Loan Model of Interest with or without the Social Contrivance of Money, *Journal of Political Economy*, 66(6), pp. 467.

Sargent, T. (1982). The Ends of Four Big Inflations, in R. E. Hall (ed.), *Inflation: Causes and Effects*, National Bureau of Economic Research, pp. 41–98.

Sargent, T. J. and F. R. Velde, (2002). *The Big Problem of Small Change*, Princeton, NJ: Princeton University Press.

Sargent, T. J. and N. Wallace, (1976). Rational Expectations and the Theory of Economic Policy, *Journal of Monetary Economics*, 2(2), pp. 169–183.

Sargent, T. J. S., (1982). The Ends of Four Big Inflations, in Robert E. Hall (ed.), *Inflation: Causes and Effects*. Chicago: University of Chicago Press (for National Bureau of Economic Research).

Sayers, R. S., (1957). *Central Banking after Bagehot*, London: Oxford University Press.

Shirras, F. G. and J. H. Craig, (1945). Sir Isaac Newton and the Currency, *The Economic Journal*, 55, pp. 217–241.

Shrimplin, V., (2017). *Sir Thomas Gresham and His Vision for Gresham College*, London: Pitkin Publishing.

Sinclair, P. and Allen, W. A. (2017). Monetary Policy Normals, Future and Past, *National Institute Economic Review*, 241(1), R5–R12.

Solow, R. M., (1987). Growth Theory and After, lecture in memory of Alfred Nobel, 8 December, www.nobelprize.org/nobel_prizes/economic-sciences/laureates/1987/solow-lecture.html.

Spufford, P., (1988). *Money and Its Use in Medieval Europe*, Cambridge: Cambridge University Press.

Stark, J., (2008). Why Money Data Are Vital to the Eurozone, *Financial Times*, 26 May.

Stewart, M., (1991). *Keynes and After*, London: Penguin.

Svensson, L. E. O., (2009). Flexible Inflation Targeting – Lessons from the Financial Crisis, comments at Netherlands Bank, Amsterdam, 21 September.

Svensson, L. E. O., (2009). Flexible Inflation Targeting: Lessons from the Financial Crisis, speech at Netherlands Bank.

Swanson, E., (2011). Let's Twist Again: A High-Frequency Event-Study Analysis of Operation Twist and Its Implications for QE2. Brookings Papers on Economic Activity.

Theil, H., (1957). *Optimal Decision Rules for Government and Industry*, Amsterdam: North-Holland, 1964.

Tinbergen, J., (1966). *Economic Policy: Principles and Design*. Amsterdam: North-Holland.

Tobin, J. (1969). A General Equilibrium Approach to Monetary Theory, *Journal of Money, Credit and Banking*, 1(1), pp. 15–29.

Ugai, H., (2007). Effects of the Quantitative Easing Policy: A Survey of Empirical Analyses, *Monetary and Economic Studies, Institute for Monetary and Economic Studies*, Bank of Japan, 25(1), pp. 1–48.

Voltaire, (1789, [1972]). *Candide*, Paris: Librairie Marcel Didier.

Walsh, C., (1995). Optimal Contracts for Central Bankers, *American Economic Review*, 85, pp. 150–167.

White, W., (2006). Procyclicality in the Financial System: Do We Need a New Macrofinancial Stabilisation Framework?, BIS working paper 193.

Woodford, M., (2005). Central Bank Communication and Policy Effectiveness, paper prepared for Jackson Hole.

Woodford, M., (2007). Does a 'Two-Pillar Phillips Curve' Justify a Two-Pillar Monetary Strategy, paper presented at Fourth ECB Central Banking Conference.

Index

9 781108 838610